LEIBSTANDARTE
Hitler's Elite Bodyguard

Front cover: Re-enactor showing off the uniform of a *Leibstandarte* Pànzergrenadier in front of a Russian T-34 tank. See page 67. *Peter Amodio*

Right: What the well-dressed Waffen-SS Panzergrenadier wore while digging on the Eastern Front in April 1944. He has a camouflaged helmet cover, camouflaged battledress, belt with M36 buckle, two triple sets of Model 1911 rifle ammunition pouches, from which two *Eiergranaten 39* hand grenades are suspended, and an S84/98 bayonet at his side. *All photographs in this book — unless specifically credited otherwise — are provided from the Brian L. Davis collection*

SPEARHEAD

LEIBSTANDARTE
Hitler's Elite Bodyguard

Michael Sharpe & Brian L. Davis

Ian Allan
60th
ANNIVERSARY

Abbreviations

AC	Armoured car
Arty	Artillery
Atk	Anti-tank
Bn	Battalion
Brig	Brigade
Bty	Battery
Coy	Company
Engr	Engineer
FBK	*Führerbegleit-kommando*
Hy	Heavy
leFH	*leichte Feldhaubitze* (light field gun)
LAH/LSSAH	*Leibstandarte-SS Adolf Hitler*
Lt	Lieutenant; light
MC	Motorcycle
Mor	Mortar
Mot	Motorised
NSDAP	*Nationalsozialistische Deutsche Arbeiterpartei* (Nazi party)
OKW	*Oberkommando der Wehrmacht*
OKH	*Oberkommando des Heeres*
Pak	*Panzerabwehrkanone* (anti-tank gun)
Pl	Platoon
PzBefWag	*Panzerbefehls-wagen* (armd comd vehicle)
PzGr	*Panzergrenadier*
PzJr	*Panzerjäger*
PzKpfw	*Panzerkampfwagen* tank
RHQ	Regimental HQ
SA	*Sturmabteilung*
Sect	Section
Sig	Signals
SP	Self-propelled
SS	*Schutzstaffel*
Tk	Tank
WH	*Wehrmacht Heer* (as in car and MC numberplates)

Dates

20/7/54	20 July 1954

First published 2002

ISBN 0 7110 2922 9

© Compendium Publishing 2002

Published by Ian Allan Publishing

an imprint of Ian Allan Publishing Ltd, Hersham, Surrey KT12 4RG.
Printed by Ian Allan Printing Ltd, Hersham, Surrey KT12 4RG.

Code: 0209/A2

British Library Cataloguing in Publication Data
A CIP catalogue record for this book is available from the British Library

SS Ranks

Mannschaften (Enlisted men)
SS-Schütze
SS-Oberschütze
SS-Sturmmann
SS-Rottenführer
SS-Stabsrottenführer

Unteroffiziere ohne Portepee (Junior NCOs)
SS-Unterscharführer
SS-Standartenjunker

Unteroffiziere mit Portepee (Senior NCOs)
SS-Oberscharführer
SS-Hauptscharführer
SS-Sturmscharführer

Offiziere (Commissioned Officers)
SS-Untersturmführer
SS-Obersturmführer
SS-Hauptsturmführer
SS-Sturmbannführer
SS-Obersturmbannführer
SS-Standartenführer
SS-Brigadeführer und Generalmajor der Waffen-SS
SS-Gruppenführer und Generalleutnant der Waffen-SS
SS-Obergruppenführer und General der Waffen-SS
SS-Oberstgruppenführer und Generaloberst der Waffen-SS
Reichsführer-SS

Waffen-SS formations/unit structure

Abteilung Similar to a battalion, a formation of combined units designed to be independent on the battlefield.

Armee (army) Comprised of several Korps, plus any independent formations the *Armee* operated on the strategic level. The only Waffen-SS *Armee* was Sixth SS-Panzer Army.

Aufklärung (reconnaissance) Waffen-SS recce units were well-armed and had two coys of ACs, plus several MC coys and a motorised heavy weapons coy.

Bataillon (battalion) Tactical unit of three or more *Kompanien*, sometimes with additional *Züge* and a strength of between 500–1,000 soldiers.

Batterie (battery) A group of support weapons operating as a unit.

Brigade Independent formation, usually of 1-7,000 soldiers. Most Waffen-SS brigades and/or legions were foreign volunteer units of varying size and thus not relevant to the *Leibstandarte*.

Division Combination of several regiments and *Abteilungen*, with manpower of anything between 10–21,000 soldiers. Waffen-SS panzer divisions tended to have a large complement.

Feldersatz (field replacement) When possible, Waffen-SS divisions would have an *Ersatz*, or replacement formation, often in Germany, which fed new troops to the front line units.

Feldpostamt (FPA) Military post office.

CONTENTS

Flak (AA) units usually had a mixture of towed heavy 88mm, motorised med 37mm and lt 20mm quad AA guns.

Kolonne (column) An independent transportation unit, varying in size, transporting equipment or supplies such as a bridge column or a light infantry column (which consisted of a number of horse-drawn vehicles capable of transporting a fixed tonnage).

Kommando (detachment) Tactical military formation of indeterminate size.

Kompanie (company) Tactical unit of three or more *Züge*, with a strength of 100–200 soldiers.

Korps (corps) Ideally the Waffen-SS corps (formed from 1943) comprised two or more divisions, plus several attached *Abteilungen*, and the HQ staff. Although the I SS Panzer Korps was the model, manpower shortages meant that the size and quality of each varied.

Nachrichten (signals) A signals unit, comprised *Fernsprech* (telephone), *Funk* (radio) and a *Versorgungs* units.

Nachschubtruppe Supply troops, which included non-combatants such as the veterinary unit, the *Backerie-Kompanie*

(bakery), *Fleischerei* (butcher), news and QM units.

Panzer (armour) Tank battalions were organised into companies, with one or more command (*Befehl*) tanks per company, and *Werkstatt* (workshop/ repair) and *Versorgungs* companies allocated to each regiment. Each Pz Div had attached a deep-maintenance *Kraftfahrzeug* detachment, including a workshop, weapons and a spares unit.

Panzerjäger (anti-tank) A PzJg unit usually contained a mixture of motorised and stationary anti-tank weapons.

Pionier (assault engineers) In addition to building bridges and fortifications, *Pionier* troops were trained as assault troops, specialising in urban fighting and weapons like flamethrowers and satchel charges. Usually split into an armoured company, several *Pionier* and special companies such as *Brücken* (bridging) and assault boat.

Regiment Comprising several *Bataillone*, with anywhere between 2–6,000 men.

Sanitätstruppe (medical troops) These included the *Feldlazarett* (field hospital unit), comprising the *Sanitäts* companies

and the *Krankenkraftwagen* (motorised ambulance) section.

Stab (staff) Headquarters unit comprising officers who would be assigned to a specific role such as: Ia = operations; Ib = supply & transport; Ic = intelligence; Id = training; IIa = personnel matters, officers; IIb = personnel matters, men; III = judge advocate; IVa = administration; IVb = medical; V = motor transport. Div HQ included the CO, plus staff officers, cartographers (*Kartenstelle*), a signals unit, an MP unit (*Feldgendarmerie*), plus an escort force and transport team.

Trupp (troop) Tactical, sometimes independent, unit of 10–20 men.

Werfer (mortar) Compared to Allied formations, German units were much better armed with mortars. A divisional *Werfer* unit typically had three batteries of six 150mm towed mortars and a battery of six 210mm towed mortars. After 1943 six battalions of SS *Nebeltruppen* (specialised rocket launcher troops) were raised and equipped with *Nebelwerfer* (a multi-barrelled rocket launcher).

Zug (platoon; plural *Züge*) A tactical unit of 30–40 soldiers.

ORIGINS & HISTORY

The 1st SS-Panzer Division *Leibstandarte*-SS Adolf Hitler was the first armed SS formation and, by most measures, the most capable. Based from the early 1930s at Lichterfelde Kaserne (barracks), Berlin, its troops were the standard-bearers of the fledgling SS, although initially they were referred to contemptuously by army regulars as the 'asphalt soldiers' for their obsessive spit and polish drill and purely ceremonial duties. After the campaigns in Poland and France, contempt gave way to genuine respect as *Leibstandarte* earned its reputation as a combat unit, which lived, as one *Leibstandarte* captain later reflected, for the 'sheer beauty of the fighting'.

EARLY HISTORY

The history of the *Leibstandarte* is inextricably tied to that of the Waffen-SS, the military wing of the *Schutzstaffel* (SS). Its early origins, therefore, lay in the men who provided protection for the leaders of the fledgling *Nationalsozialistische Deutsche Arbeiterpartei* — the National Socialist German Workers' Party, or Nazis — in the often violent political scene of Germany of the 1920s and 1930s . These bodyguards were first drawn from the party's Sports and Gymnastics Section, which later grew into the Sturmabteilung (SA) under the leadership of Ernst Röhm.

The year 1923 saw the formation of the *Stabswache* (Headquarters Guard), a rather grandiose title for what was, in reality, just two men acting as bodyguards to Hitler. The creation of this unit, the first such body dedicated to the personal protection of the Führer, was motivated by Hitler's growing mistrust of the SA, the ranks of which were filled with former Freikorps volunteers and members of the Brigade Ehrhardt, a right-wing organisation whose eponymous leader was openly contemptuous of Hitler. Hitler's fears were soon confirmed when Ehrhardt withdrew his men from the SA, and the Stabswache was disbanded. Realising that he needed to exercise greater control over the SA, Hitler appointed his trusted comrade Göring to lead it, but despite Göring's success in restructuring the unit

Below: The newly formed '*Stosstrupp* Hitler', the Adolf Hitler Shock Troop, leaving for the German Day (*Deutscher Tag*) held in Bayreuth on 2 September 1923. These early German Day gatherings were the precursors of the huge Nuremberg *Parteitagen* (Party Days), the largest of which was that held on 5–12 September 1938.

STOSSTRUPP-HITLER
MÜNCHEN

the gulf between the SA and party leadership continued to grow. Subsequently, the *Stosstrupp* (Shock Troop) Adolf Hitler was formed from men whose personal loyalty to Hitler was beyond question. Among its members was Josef 'Sepp' Dietrich, the most famous of *Leibstandarte* commanders, and Rudolf Hess, who rose to be Deputy Leader of the Nazi Party.

In November, along with the numerically superior SA, the *Stosstrupp* participated in the failed Munich Beer Hall Putsch, the NSDAP's ill-conceived and semi-farcical attempt to wrest control of Germany by coup d-état. At least 12 *Stosstrupp* members were shot down and killed around the Nazi leaders as they marched at the head of an army of rebels. While Hitler languished in Landsberg prison for his part in the coup, the various factions of the now-outlawed and leaderless party became divided. The SA, also banned by law, was reorganised by Ernst Röhm into the *Frontbann*, and by the time that Hitler was released, it boasted some 30,000 members. Such visible growth in Röhm's power concerned Hitler greatly, and he was soon in dispute with the Röhm and the *Frontbann*, members of which had begun to openly criticise Hitler's leadership.

Above: Berlin, 30 January 1938. To mark the fifth anniversary of the National Socialists coming to power, a parade was held in front of the Reich Chancellery in the Wilhelmstrasse, Berlin. Here a contingent of the *Leibstandarte*-SS marches past Hitler, who is accompanied by — from left to right — Rudolf Hess, Deputy Leader; Sepp Dietrich, commander of the LSSAH; and Reichsführer-SS Heinrich Himmler.

CREATION OF THE SS

Hitler reacted by removing Röhm in April 1925 and that same month created the SS as a kind of praetorian guard. Initially this was comprised of only eight men, all of whom had demonstrated unswerving loyalty to Hitler. SS units, each of ten sober, healthy men with untainted criminal records, were subsequently raised in other districts, but as a gesture to the still-powerful SA they were placed under its control. The SA resented the elitism of the SS and in turn the SS was embittered by the offhand treatment it received at the hands of its SA overlords. It was also frustrated by the

Above: The *Leibstandarte*-SS Adolf Hitler marches through the streets of Nuremberg led by its commanding officer, Sepp Dietrich, during the 1935 *Reichsparteitag*.

restrictions on its numbers, while the SA, which was willing to accept almost any man, continued to expand. Control of the SS passed through the hands of two leaders in quick succession, neither of them able to stand up to the bullying of the SA. Morale among the membership declined, and with the arrival of the a new leader, Heinrich Himmler, in 1929, the SS seemed condemned to a history of mediocrity.

Few had reckoned on the relentless ambition and drive that Himmler would bring to the role of leader of the SS. His meek appearance and mild manner were interpreted as weaknesses by his party peers, but his participation in the abortive Munich putsch, fanatical devotion to the cause and loyalty to Hitler were well known. Thus this one-time chicken farmer, industrial chemist and homeopathy enthusiast became leader of the SS, and set about turning it into a unit that would rival and eventually supplant the SA as the military wing of the Nazi party.

The SS that Himmler took over had barely 280 members. He determined to expand it according to his own politico-eugenic theories, which had imbued in him a belief in the racial superiority of the Germanic race, and a desire to foster a nation of racially pure supermen, with the SS at its head. He persuaded Hitler to allow him to introduce tough membership rules, by which new members had to prove their family lineage extending back for three generations. Undesirables were ejected and discipline tightened. SS numbers grew slowly, reaching 1,000 by the end of 1929, as more and more recruits began to favour the disciplined elite status of the SS over the rowdy, loutish and drunken SA. At the end of 1930, SS membership stood at 3,000, and Himmler had successfully wrested control of the unit from the SA.

The SA had become a major problem for Hitler by this time. It had grown out of control, while the party itself had split into rival factions. The inevitable confrontation broke out in mid-1930, when the SA deputy commander demanded that Hitler reduce party interference in SA affairs. Hitler refused, brought back Ernst Röhm to replace the SA commander, Ernst von Salomon, and demanded that SA members swear an oath of allegiance to him. They refused, and by the new year the air was again thick with rumours of a plot against the leader, but when the SA attempted to take over the party in April 1931 the rank and file remained loyal to Hitler and the rebellion melted away.

SS strength rose dramatically that year, and on the eve of the elections that swept Hitler to power he could count on some 30,000 men. In March 1933, a select band of these were chosen by Oberstgruppenführer Sepp Dietrich to form the SS-*Stabswache* Berlin, the progenitor of the *Leibstandarte*, a Praetorian guard responsible for protecting Hitler.

Dietrich, a fellow Bavarian and trusted party comrade of Hitler's, created the *Stabswache* with 120 hand-picked men who were paragons of the SS ideal: 25 years old, 1.8 metres tall, and with no criminal record. On 17 March, the first unit muster was held at the Alexander Kaserne in Friedrichstrasse. In April it transferred to Lichterfelde Kaserne, Berlin, where it was retitled SS-*Sonderkommando* Berlin and a 12-man guard under Wilhelm Mohnke was posted to the Reich Chancellery. Its first published appearance as an honour guard for the Führer came during an SA rally at the Berlin Sports Palace on 8 April. The following month a special training unit, SS-*Sonderkommando* Zossen, was raised from three companies of troops to support the

---

ORGANISATION OF *LEIBSTANDARTE*-SS ADOLF HITLER REGIMENT AS OF OCTOBER 1934

Stab (HQ) with Sig Pl and Band
3 x *Sturmbanne* (mot)
  each of 3 x *Stürme* (mot),
  1 x Sig Pl and 1 x MG-*Stürme* (mot)
1 x MC *Sturm*
1 x Mortar *Sturm* (mot)
1 x Recce Pl

Note: *Sturmbann*—Storm Battalion—is the name given to SA units in the early years of Nazism. The word *Sturmbann* would disappear in unit terms but continue to be used in SS ranks such as *Sturmbannführer* (see list on page 4).

bodyguard unit. Initially, the duties of the SS-*Sonderkommando* Berlin were almost purely ceremonial. It mounted a 24-hour guard outside the Reich Chancellery and the Führer's residence in the Wilhelmstrasse. A very select group, known as the *Führerbegleitkommando* (Führer escort commando) served as Hitler's personal staff — waiters, valets, drivers and the like. Whenever he appeared in public in his famous open Mercedes, he was flanked by *Leibstandarte* troops.

A further name change came in July, when SS-*Stabswache* Berlin was renamed SS-*Sonderkommando* Jüterbog. During that summer a detachment of the FBK under Theodor 'Teddy' Wisch stood guard for the first time at Hitler's summer retreat near Berchtesgaden.

The final act of this period of reorganisation came in September 1933, when SS-*Sonderkommando* Jüterbog and SS-*Sonderkommando* Zossen combined as the Adolf Hitler *Standarte*. At Hitler's suggestion this was changed to *Leibstandarte* Adolf Hitler, a name redolent of the old Imperial Bavarian Life Guards. The name was enshrined at the September *Parteitag* rally, for which the *Leibstandarte*, turned out in the striking jet-black SS uniform, provided the honour guard. Another significant event was the official swearing in of the men at a ceremony on 9 November to mark the tenth anniversary of the Beer Hall Putsch. It was held at the Feldherrnhalle War Memorial, in Munich's Odeonplatz. The highlights of the ceremony, full of pomp and pageantry, were a recantation by torchlight of the SS oath of allegiance to the Führer by some 835 LAH members, and the presentation of the first regimental colours.

Such spectacles, and the presence of its troops outside the Chancellery, Berlin's three airports, various ministries (including SS headquarters), as well as the private homes of the Führer and Reichsführer-SS Heinrich Himmler, had helped the *Leibstandarte* Adolf Hitler (the 'SS' was inserted later) quickly to gain for itself a very public profile. Its role would soon extend, however, into the darker corners of the Nazi regime.

Above: Adolf Hitler, chancellor since 30 January 1933, addresses a political meeting held in the Berlin Sports Palace on 8 April of that year. This photograph shows the meeting being guarded by full-time armed and steel-helmeted members of the newly formed SS-*Stabswache* Berlin. Six months later, by then named the SS-*Sonderkommando* Jüterbog, the unit was once more retitled, this time at the 1933 Nuremberg *Parteitag* Rally, becoming the Adolf Hitler *Standarte*.

NIGHT OF THE LONG KNIVES

The threat posed by the half-million SA members to Hitler's dominance emerged again in early 1934. Its leadership and many of the rank and file had become disillusioned with the Nazi party, which they felt had become too much a part of the establishment that the socialist-orientated SA sought to overthrow. When Röhm expressed these reservations in a speech in February 1934 and demanded a greater role for the SA in Germany's future, Hitler moved quickly.

On 30 June, the so-called 'Night of the Long Knives', Hitler, Dietrich and a six-man LAH escort travelled to Bad Wiesee, where a conference of senior SA officers was to take place, with. They arrested Ernst Röhm and other SA leaders, taking them to Stadelheim prison where they were executed by an LAH firing squad. In Berlin, LAH units were even more active, arresting more SA men and other political enemies whom the Nazis wanted eliminated. It is difficult to be precise about the number killed by firing squad: the figure was well over 100. The decapitated SA was disarmed and the power of the organisation faded rapidly. SS fortunes, by contrast, were very much in the ascendant.

READY FOR WAR

In the mid-1930s the military forces of the Third Reich were expanded to ready them for Hitler's campaigns of conquest. Under this expansion both the army and the SS dramatically increased their strength, and by September 1939 the German armed forces were certainly the most disciplined, highly trained and best equipped in the world.

From the outset Himmler had desired a separate armed force for the SS, and he pushed and won approval for the creation of separate paramilitary units under the jurisdiction of the SS. Of course, there already existed two armed units — the *Leibstandarte* was one; the other were the *Totenkopfverbände* (Death's Head units) that guarded the concentration camps — the first three, set up in 1933 were Dachau, Buchenwald and Sachsenhausen — purpose-built to detain those accused of political and ideological crimes against the Reich. With the downfall of the SA in 1934 the SS took over camp administration. The *Totenkopfverbände* were subsequently reorganised by Theodor Eicke and would go on to form the core of the *Totenkopf* division.

However, Himmler had greater ambitions for the men that he had preached in 1931 would be the 'Gods of the new Germany'. On 16 March 1935, Hitler announced the formation of the SS-*Verfügungstruppen* (special purpose troops). The SS-VT was created by amalgamating established SS-*Politische Bereitschaften* (political readiness squads) into three regiments each with engineer and signals battalions. These formed the core of what became in 1940 the Waffen-SS, or armed SS. For administrative purposes, the *Leibstandarte* was considered to be part of this body, and although it was often preoccupied with ceremonial duties, received much of its early military training from SS-VT troops.

The SS-VT was distinct from other arms of the SS, although the two organisations mingled. It was expected to be a military organisation completely obedient and loyal to its master, Adolf Hitler, but its purpose was never entirely clear, since national defence was already in the hands of the Wehrmacht. Himmler and Hitler never came up with a satisfactory answer, usually referring to the SS-VT as a *Weltanschauliche Truppen* or 'political soldiers' that served Hitler directly as 'the spearhead of National Socialism'. In reality, its purpose was to carry out whatever task Hitler and Himmler demanded; its existence became Himmler's justification for the continued growth of the SS.

In mid-1934 the *Leibstandarte* added SS to its official name, the abbreviation changing to LSSAH. Correspondingly its duties were expanded and the unit was reorganised along military lines. Between October and December 1934, it re-equipped as a motorised unit and by the end of November it consisted of three battalions, a motorcycle company, a mortar company, an armoured car platoon and a signals platoon. In addition it maintained a band. At the time of the reoccupation

of the Saarland in February 1935, the *Leibstandarte* had a strength of around 2,500 men, or a quarter of the SS total. On Hitler's triumphant motorised parade into Saarbrücken, LSSAH provided the escort, much to the chagrin of the Wehrmacht, and on 1 March it was again in the spotlight at the head of the forces reoccupying the Rhineland.

Hostilities between the conservative, rigidly class-conscious regular army — *das Heer* — and the upstart armed SS formations reached a new height in 1935, and although Hitler was quick to play down the independent military role of the SS for fear of ostracising the army, the antagonism continued. Within the confines of the SS, *Leibstandarte* commander Sepp Dietrich's personal relationship with Himmler, who could intimidate most of his subordinates, was also less than cordial, and the two were frequently at odds.

The Waffen-SS and the Wehrmacht differed in many, many respects — political motivation, allegiance and structure among them. Less obviously, SS men were from predominantly rural backgrounds and had received less schooling than their Wehrmacht counterparts, although they had to conform to higher physical standards. *Leibstandarte* entry requirements were particularly stringent; in fact, before regulations were relaxed men were routinely rejected for having just a single tooth filled! Rapid expansion of the army to 35 divisions after 1936 forced the army to lower certain conditions of recruitment, and in turn it limited the number of conscripts it would allow to join the SS.

Hitler's territorial ambitions had been far from satisfied by the reoccupation of former German territories in 1935, and he viewed it as the birthright of the German people to expand further, occupying 'Lebensraum' populated by 'lesser' races. Such expansion clearly required a strong military force, which Hitler began slowly building since 1933. The expansion of all branches of the military, in flagrant disregard for the Versailles Treaty that outlawed any such expansion, included the SS. Under Reichsführer-

Above: Members of the SS-VT inspect the result of their musketry practice. Note the SS runes on the sides of their Model 1916 helmets. The old Model 1916 was used until the end of the war — albeit mainly by Volkssturm personnel — despite being replaced on 1 July 1935 by a lighter, redesigned issue.

Above: An SdKfz 7 halftrack is put through its paces. The SdKfz 7 was the most numerous German halftrack — 12,000 units were built between 1938 and 1944 — that was mainly used as artillery prime mover, with an eight-ton haulage capacity. Variants carried quad 20mm or single 37mm Flak guns. 1944.

SS Himmler this was growing into a vast self-contained political apparatus — the shining star of the Nazi regime — with interests that extended into economic, military and social spheres.

The SS-VT, the military wing, had emerged with great prestige from the occupation of the Saarland, but its precise role in any future conflict was somewhat muddled, and despite the undoubtedly high physical qualities of its soldiers, it lacked combat experience. The first problem stemmed from the fact that, although it had ostensibly been established as a 'permanent armed force at (Hitler's) disposal', he had also publicly stated on numerous occasions that the SS-VT would, in time of war, be attached to the regular army and fight as soldiers under its command in defence of Germany. Thus its role appeared to overlap with that of the Wehrmacht, which resented any such intrusion on its territory. Privately, Hitler expressed his feelings that it was necessary for the SS to prove itself in combat, in order to secure the confidence and respect of the population.

So to Himmler he entrusted the recruiting and training — both military and ideological — of the SS-VT, and in 1936 he appointed an experienced former Wehrmacht officer, Paul Hausser, to the Inspectorate of the SS-VT. With his subordinates Felix Steiner and Cassius Freiherr von Montigny, Hausser devised a tough and thorough training programme for the SS-VT regiments, involving weapons and unarmed combat training, and particular emphasis was placed on physical training. Exercises were frequently conducted using live ammunition. Additionally, the SS soldier was subjected to frequent lectures on Nazi politics, racial superiority and the like. The same programme was adapted to the *Leibstandarte*, which conducted its training at the grandiose Lichterfelde barracks,

Right: Hitler on a tour of inspection of the SS barracks, Christmas 1935. Hitler is seen with Dietrich inspecting the contents of a young soldier's locker.

although it already had a busy ceremonial schedule to fulfil.

One such public duty for the *Leibstandarte* was the honour guard for the 1936 Winter Olympics, a role it repeated at the Summer Olympics in Berlin. Both events were heralded as a showcase for the 'miracle' of National Socialism, but Hitler's true intentions for the Germany were at that very moment being played out behind closed doors.

He had since 1933 been courting Austrian voters and expressing his desire to unite the countries under one leader. He had already, in 1934, backed a failed coup d'état by the Austrian Nazi Party to overthrow the government. In the aftermath hundreds of Nazi were jailed, but were soon released to begin scheming once more. Hitler continued the pressure on the national government through sympathisers in the Austrian assembly, and in 1938, the final year of peace under the Third Reich, he began another phase of expansion that ultimately led to war, brief glory and, after six long years, defeat.

For the March occupation of Austria — the Anschluss — the *Leibstandarte* was under General Heinz Guderian's XVI Army Corps, and provided an escort for Hitler as he rode in triumph to the Austrian capital. Here it stayed until April under the command of 2nd Panzer Division, and then returned to Berlin.

In April Hitler ordered planning to begin for *Fall Grün* (Operation Green), the occupation of the Sudetenland, a mountainous area between Bohemia and Silesia where 3.25 million Germans were living under Czech rule. At the end of September, after manoeuvring around the British and French at Munich, Hitler was able to occupy the Sudetenland. For the operation, *Leibstandarte* was again attached to the XVIth Army Corps and it was achieved without

incident. Further appeased, he bullied and cajoled the Czech government to renounce the country's independence and accept status as a German protectorate. When they agreed, Hitler moved quickly and in mid-March 1939 sent troops in to occupy the remaining Czechoslovak territories. This, too, was achieved without incident, but the increasingly active role of the SS (all three SS regiments took part in the Czech operations), and the fact that they were now wearing the same field grey uniforms as the army, did not please the OKW.

Above: Men of the SS parade in the Luitpold Arena, Nuremberg, 13 September 1936. Following on from the militarism of the 1935 rally, the 1936 rally showed the results of rearmament — tanks, armoured cars and aircraft. The massed ranks of the SS, 250,000 party members, and 70,000 spectators watched Hitler tell the world that the Third Reich would last a thousand years. The Luitpoldhain was so named for an old Bavarian monarch, an exhibition park that was laid out in 1906.

A month later there was a return to official duties when Hitler opened the 7km Tiergartenstrasse in an official ceremony honouring his 50th birthday. With *Leibstandarte* troops lining the road as the Honour Guard, the Führer drove the length of the spectacular new highway in his open Mercedes. Emboldened by the weakness he perceived in the British and French, he was already planning the next stage of conquest, into Poland, and in January had already renewed his demands for the return of Danzig.

IN ACTION

POLAND — *Fall Weiss*

For Germans of all political leanings the Republic of Poland and the Danzig Corridor that divided the territory of East Prussia from the rest of Germany were constant and bitter reminders of the humiliation meted out by the Treaty of Versailles at the end of World War I.

In January 1939, following his diplomatic successes of 1938, Hitler began to demand that the territories be fully restored to Germany. The demands were rebuffed but, encouraged by the continuing British and French posture of appeasement, on 3 April he ordered the *Oberkommando der Wehrmacht* (OKW) to formulate plans for an attack. He remained, however, fearful of antagonising the Soviets, and so forged an unlikely alliance with that country on 23 August — the Molotov-Ribbentrop Pact. This secretly divided Eastern Europe into German and Soviet spheres of influence, allowed for the attack on Poland and the splitting of the territory gained between the two countries.

Newly schooled in the tactics of Blitzkrieg, the OKH planned to use maximum surprise in the attack, codenamed *Fall Weiss* (Operation White). Some 98 Wehrmacht divisions were mobilised in preparation for the offensive, and throughout July and early August these units moved quietly to positions on both sides of Germany — to the east on the Polish border ready to invade, and to the west to take up defensive positions to meet the anticipated counter-attack by the British and French. In the north General Fedor von Bock's Fourth Army was to attack from Pomerania; the Third Army, also under command of Bock's Army Group North, would advance from East Prussia on the other arm of a giant pincer movement. In the south Generaloberst Gerd von Rundstedt's Eighth (Blaskowitz) and Tenth (von Reichenau) Armies would strike from Silesia toward Warsaw, and the Fourteenth Army (List) would move on Krakow in the south-west to cut off any Polish retreat.

Below: Accompanied by members of his military staff and his personal SS bodyguard, Hitler is cheered on by enthusiastic German soldiers during a visit he made to the front in Poland in 1939.

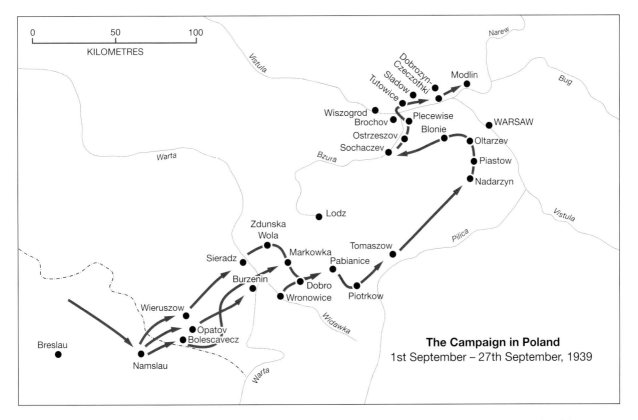

Above: *Leibstandarte*'s part in the Polish campaign, 1–27 September 1939. In spite of criticism by regular army units, the regiment was involved in intense fighting and performed creditably.

Leibstandarte had been preparing for the campaign since June, and in August had received orders to move from Lichterfelde Barracks to an assembly area around Hundsfeld-Kunersdorf east of Berlin. The OKW remained highly sceptical of SS abilities away from the parade ground, yet had little option but to acquiesce to Hitler's wishes that the SS be included in the attack. *Leibstandarte*, therefore, was attached to XIII Corps, part of Johannes Blaskowitz's Eighth Army in Army Group South, tasked with defending the left flank of Walther von Reichenau's Tenth Army, which was to drive east in a two-pronged movement to cut off the Polish forces west of Warsaw. During the initial advance the *Leibstandarte*, being a fully motorised unit, was to come under the control of 17th Infantry Division and was tasked with reconnaissance forward and the defence of the slower moving army units.

For the attack on Poland *Leibstandarte*'s main units comprised three motorised infantry battalions, transported in trucks; a motorcycle company; an engineer platoon; and a section of armoured reconnaissance vehicles. This unit was under the command of Kurt Meyer, who renamed it 'Panzer Meyer' before the assault on Poland. (The nickname would stick and he would be 'Panzer' Meyer henceforth.) It is worth noting that many of the officers commanding *Leibstandarte* units during this campaign would go on to become respected commanders later in the war.

Shortly before 01:00hrs on 1 September some 37 German divisions began to move from their start points toward the German–Polish border. By dawn the *Leibstandarte*, advancing south of Breslau, was crossing at River Prosna at Gola, over a bridge lightly defended by the Polish 10th Infantry Division. The Polish Army, with a potential strength of 1,800,000 men, was not an insignificant force, yet most of its weaponry was of World War I vintage and the Polish General Staff had dispersed this force along the whole frontier, rather than concentrate it at the most gravely threatened points.

Above: Men of a Waffen-SS assault troop advancing against an enemy position. The original caption implies that this is during action in Poland, although it's more likely to be during training for Fall Weiss. It gives a good view of the sort of equipment carried into battle — including bayonet, entrenching tool and a spare machine gun barrel within the tubular container.

From Gola the advance into Poland was rapid; Boleslavecz fell quickly, and despite spirited counter-attacks by the Polish 10th, 17th and 25th Infantry Divisions, and the mounted troops of the Wielpolska and Wolwyska Cavalry Brigades, *Leibstandarte* had almost achieved all its objectives by the afternoon of the first day. Advancing through Opatov along the Prosna River, finally, by the evening of 1st, the bulk of the regiment was across the river and preparing to advance on Wieuroszov, where it was to link up with the 17th Division. This was accomplished, and early the next morning troops of the *Leibstandarte* advanced towards Burzenin, where it was ordered to assault across the Warta River. Fierce resistance brought a frustrating delay and casualties.

On 7 September elements of Tenth Army advanced north-east to within 30 miles of Warsaw, in the first move of a double pincer envelopment, and succeeded in cutting off Polish forces before they could retreat behind the Vistula. The Eighth Army succeeded in taking Lodz, 75 miles south-east of Warsaw, that same day. *Leibstandarte* moved next on the transport hub of Pabianice, 10 miles south-west of Lodz near the Pilica River. The 1st Battalion was to isolate Pabianice from the north, while the 2nd Battalion would move south and the 3rd Battalion would remain in reserve with the artillery along the highway. The army lent a little support; a company from 17th Infantry Division and some armour (PzKpfw IIFs) from 23rd Panzer Regiment . To the north, 1st Battalion encountered no great opposition and secured its objectives quickly. To the south, however, the 2nd Battalion had to capture and hold a second highway running into Lodz, but well-sited dug-outs and stubborn defence slowed the advance, as Polish reinforcements were thrown into the battle. In the face of fierce counter-attacks from woods south of the scene of action, at one point the *Leibstandarte* seemed threatened with encirclement and was only saved by the timely intervention of Infantry Regiment 55.

Early on the 8th Pabianice fell, but for all its efforts the *Leibstandarte* was severely criticised by Generalmajor Loch, commander of the 17th Division, for forcing the diversion of 55th Infantry Regiment at a crucial juncture. He demanded its withdrawal to the reserve, and although his demand was not met, the unit was subsequently quietly transferred to Reinhardt's 4th Panzer Division.

With the route to Warsaw now wide open, von Reichenau's Tenth Army turned its axis of advance north and advanced toward the capital from the south-west, while the Fourth Army closed from the north. Guderian's armoured corps advancing from the north-west met with Ewald von Kleist's armour moving from the south at Brest-Litovsk on the 14th, effectively cutting off any potential escape route.

On the western approaches 1st Battalion of *Leibstandarte*, now reinforced by artillery, fought bitterly to wrest Oltarzev from its stalwart defenders. However although battered, the Poles were far from beaten, and had declared Warsaw a fortress. Instead of withdrawing east to escape the pincer movement, on 10 September the Polish commander, Marshal Edward Smigdly-Rydz, ordered a retreat to south-east Poland and struck south at the Eighth Army, that was protecting the northern flanks of the Tenth Army. The Polish attack temporarily threw the Germans off balance; on the outskirts of the city counter-attacks against *Leibstandarte*, fighting alongside the 4th Panzer Division, forced it onto the defensive and wiped out the 6th Company of the 2nd Battalion. Withdrawn to the west, it was attached to the forces attempting to encircle the Polish forces on the Bzura.

Von Reichenau had positioned his Tenth Army on the Bzura River, which flows into the Vistula to the north of Warsaw, and on the 14th began a northward drive to seal off the Bzura 'pocket'. Under XVI Corps, *Leibstandarte* played a major part in this operation, which was the largest battle of the Polish campaign. Some of the heaviest fighting took place in the streets of Sochaczev, where *Leibstandarte* encountered strong resistance. The Battle of Bzura was distinguished by the great bravery of the trapped Polish forces, by now facing annihilation, but finally on the 19th the jaws closed around them. In truth, the Soviet Union had delivered the death knell when it began its invasion of Eastern Poland on the 17th.

After the defeat at Bzura, all attention now focused on beleaguered Warsaw and its surrounding garrison forts. Guarding the northern approaches, the forts of Modlin and Zacrozym were attacked by battle groups from the SS-*Standarte Deutschland*, while in the centre the *Leibstandarte*, attached to XV Corps, moved on Warsaw from the west. The reduction of the forts by German artillery, aided by Luftwaffe bombers, was completed by 25 September, and two days later the Polish commander of the city sued for peace.

On 30 September, as the remaining Polish forces were mopped up, the *Leibstandarte* was awarded a special standard in light of the heavy casualties it had suffered during the campaign. In the aftermath of the Polish campaign, army commanders were quick to criticise SS units. Indeed, casualties had been inordinately high among the three SS-VT units that had served in Poland. *Leibstandarte* alone suffered more than 400 killed, wounded or missing. This, the army believed, was proof that the SS was poorly led and trained, and reckless in the attack to boot. The SS countered that the OKW had consistently used the SS for the most dangerous tasks, and that the practice of dividing SS units among army formations (only *Leibstandarte* fought as a cohesive unit) was detrimental to their effectiveness in battle. Additionally, the OKW was incensed by reported atrocities against Polish civilians, particularly Jews, by SS men, but its attempts to bring the culprits to justice were frustrated. (It should be noted that Wehrmacht personnel were also hardly guilt-free on this score.)

Overall, through their ability to redeploy rapidly from one sector of the fighting to another, the *Leibstandarte* had proved the effectiveness of motorised units in battle. This proved of vital importance in the Russian campaign.

CZECHOSLOVAKIA

During October, with most German units massed in western Europe poised for an expected attack by the British and French, the *Leibstandarte* relieved SS-*Standarte Der Führer* on its occupation duties in Czechoslovakia and paused for rest and relaxation. November and December passed quietly, and no attack came in the west, and some of the regiment was able to enjoy a peaceful Christmas at home. On 23 December Hitler joined the 1st Company for its Christmas celebration dinner at Bad Elms, Germany, at which gifts of tobacco, cake and wine were presented to each man.

ORGANISATION OF *LEIBSTANDARTE*-SS ADOLF HITLER REGIMENT IN 1940
1st *Sturmbann*
2nd *Sturmbann*
each of 3 x *Stürme*, 1 x MG *Sturm*
3rd *Sturmbann*
3 x *Stürme*, 1 x MG *Sturm*, 1 x lt Inf Gun *Sturm*, 1 x PzJg *Sturm*, 1 x MC Sturm, 1 x hy Inf Gun *Sturm*
4th Guard Battalion (later *Wachtruppe* Berlin)
Artillery Regiment (3 batteries of 10.5cm guns)
Panzer-Späh-Zug (Armd Recce Pl)
Nachrichtenzug (Sig Pl)
Kradmeldezug (MC Messenger Pl)
Kraderkundungszug (MC Recce Pl)
Pionierzug (Pionier Pl)
Panzer–Sturm–Batterie
Musik-Zug (Band)
Leichte Infanterie Kolonne (Light infantry column that consisted of a set number of horse-drawn vehicles capable of transporting a fixed tonnage)

THE PHONEY WAR

When the campaign in Poland ended, Hitler, contrary to popular belief, did not have a clear idea of what to do next. At a 23 September conference, he raised the question of what measures should be adopted 'in case of war' with Britain and France. He decided that a siege of Britain would be made more effective if the German Navy held bases in Norway, but both the Naval staff and OKH were pessimistic about such a venture and during the October and November lull that became known as the 'Phoney War', Hitler devoted himself instead to planning the attack on Belgium and France.

In preparation for the coming offensive in the west, *Leibstandarte* began a period of intensive training at Koblenz under the command of General Heinz Guderian. This coincided with a major restructuring and expansion of the SS. Criticism of the SS performance under fire could not dissuade Hitler from ordering the creation of three new SS divisions, and the establishment of a separate recruiting office under Gottlob Berger, the *Erganzungsamt der Waffen-SS*. By recruiting ethnic Germans from occupied territories (the so-called *Volksdeutsche*), which the army was prevented by law from doing, Himmler was able to expand the SS and to avoid conflict with the army over allocation of conscripts. Thus the SS-VT, which from March 1940 officially became the Waffen-SS, was expanded to three divisions: the SS-*Verfügungs* Division (an amalgamation of the SS-*Standarten Deutschland*, *Germania* and *Der Führer* that would eventually become the 2nd SS Panzer Division *Das Reich*), the *Totenkopf* and the *Polizei*, recruited from members of the police force. In March 1940, Hitler authorized the formation of a *Leibstandarte* artillery battalion armed with 105mm guns.

By the spring, growing signs that the British and French would intervene in Norway and Denmark persuaded Hitler that he, too, must act and ordered landings for 9 April. In the run-up to the invasion, the regiment was put on standby alert, but again there was no counter-punch by the Allied armies, swollen by now to 148 divisions of French (100), British (11), Belgian (22) and Dutch (10) troops. Denmark fell in a day, and although resistance in Norway continued until June, most of the country was in German control by the middle of April.

Below: Waffen-SS troops seen during the fighting in France. The soldier on the right is firing a Luger pistol complete with shoulder stock. The Pistole 08 was of World War I vintage and in its long-barrelled version could be attached to a wooden stock that allowed it to be used as a machine-pistol. The man on left carries a 7.92mm Karabiner 98b, with its side sling and sword bayonet mounted.

INVASION OF THE LOW COUNTRIES — *Fall Gelb*

The diversion in Norway somewhat delayed preparations for the next phase of German conquest — into France and the Low Countries of Holland and Belgium, but by early May these had almost been completed. The strategic plan OKH had prepared for the coming offensive, *Fall Gelb* (Operation Yellow), was itself modelled on the old Schlieffen Plan of 1914. For the battle three army groups — A, B and C under Gerd von Rundstedt, Fedor von Bock and Wilhelm von Leeb respectively — were created. The main effort would be made by Bock and von Leeb through Belgium either side of Liège, where the Belgian Army was concentrated on a defensive line on the Albert Canal and Meuse River, to seize the strategically important fortress at Eben Emael. This was much as the Allied commanders predicted, believing that an attack in north-eastern France against the formidable defences of the Maginot Line, a belt of fortifications built in the 1930s from Switzerland to Longuyon, was highly unlikely, and equally unlikely a move through the ravined and forested Ardennes region, considered impassable to armour.

The original plan called for an attack in November 1939, but after repeated postponements because of poor weather conditions, the date was firmly set for 17 January 1940. However, over the winter, Hitler and some of his strategists began to question the plan, and acting upon the suggestions of von Rundstedt *Fall Gelb* was revised. The new plan, devised by General von Manstein with the assistance of his commanding officer von Rundstedt, was based on the same Blitzkrieg tactics — the deep strategic penetration by independently operating armoured forces, with tactical air support — that had proved so effective in Poland. Under the new plan the key tank units, including the 5th and 7th Panzer Divisions under Erwin Rommel, the Kleist Armoured Group (with XIX Corps under Guderian) and the 6th and 8th Panzer Divisions under Georg-Hans Reinhardt were transferred to von Rundstedt's group (thus reducing to three the number. of armoured divisions in Bock's group). It was to make an audacious, coordinated thrust through the Ardennes and move behind the main concentration of Allied forces to Sedan, thus bypassing the Maginot Line. From there it would race to the

Above: So swift was the German advance through France and Belgium in 1940, that the exhausted troops had to snatch precious sleep whenever they could.

Below: Lying beneath the shelter of a railway wagon these men of the Waffen-SS take aim with their MG34 7.92mm machine gun.

undefended Channel coast, before turning to complete the encirclement. After it was shown to Hitler he immediately ordered it to be adopted.

For the offensive the Germans could muster some two million troops, and were thus outnumbered by the four million of the combined French, British, Dutch and Belgian armies. In tanks the Germans and Allies were roughly equal, although German tanks were generally faster, but in aircraft they enjoyed a clear advantage. The difference in opposing forces was less a question of numbers than in the way in which they were employed, and here the Germans, in their use of new methods of warfare, showed a clear advantage.

After further delays because of the weather, the assault finally began before daylight on 9 May, with extensive air attacks on the Dutch and Belgian airfields and the seizure by paratroops of vital river crossings at Moerdijk and Rotterdam. At dawn Georg von Küchler's Eighteenth Army, including the 9th Panzer Division and *Leibstandarte*, drove into Holland, the main column striking toward the southern Netherlands to envelop the southern flank of the densely populated 'Vesting Holland' (Fortress Holland) region formed by rivers and canals around the five major Dutch cities — Amsterdam, Rotterdam, Utrecht, Leiden and Den Haag — where the 400,000-man conscripted Dutch army had concentrated. *Leibstandarte*, attached to the 227th Division of Army Group B, had been given a vital role in penetrating these defences, and securing the road and river bridges along the advance to the Ijssel River after they had been captured by airborne troops of the Fallschirmjäger — 7th Flieger Division and 22nd Luftlande Division (see *Spearhead 3 7th Flieger Division*).

By midday *Leibstandarte* was 50 miles inside Dutch territory, but at Boernbrock found its progress blocked by a blown bridge. Undaunted, the regiment crossed the canal on makeshift rafts, and pressed on. Again, despite a lightning advance to Zwolle on the Ijssel, *Leibstandarte* was unable to prevent the destruction of two vital bridges there by Dutch engineers. To the south, the 3rd Battalion found another crossing point near Zutphen, and before it halted to rest that night the regiment had covered 215km (130 miles). At this juncture, *Leibstandarte* joined the 9th Panzer Division for the

drive to Rotterdam. Although German airborne troops held the key Maas (the river the French call the Meuse is the Maas in Holland) bridge at Moerdijk, to the north of the city tenacious Dutch defence had thus far prevented them from crossing. Hitler would not countenance delays and issued an ultimatum to the Dutch — capitulate or Rotterdam would be bombed. Negotiations began, but the Luftwaffe attacked anyway and destroyed the city, later citing in its defence a breakdown in communications. On 13 May, following the air raid, *Leibstandarte* was advancing through Rotterdam and was involved in an incident which later drew heavy criticism from the army. Spotting Dutch troops loitering outside a building soldiers — apparently from *Leibstandarte* — opened fire. In fact, Dutch and German officers were negotiating the surrender in the building and the fire severely wounded celebrated airborne forces' commander Karl Student. For the army, it was proof again of the indiscipline of the SS. Undeterred, Dietrich moved on and the following day *Leibstandarte* reached the Hague.

FRANCE

In response to the attack on Holland the French Seventh Army (Giraud) had moved across northern Belgium to Breda on 11 May to help the Dutch, who had fallen back from the Maas. In Belgium, the army soon fell back on a defensive line based on the defences behind the Dyle River. Holland fell on the 14th, but although it initially appeared that the Allies had succeeded in delaying the Germans here, Rundstedt had

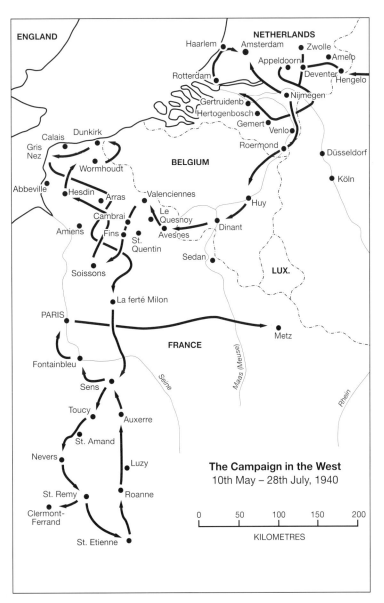

The Campaign in the West
10th May – 28th July, 1940

0	50	100	150	200

KILOMETRES

already sprung the trap on the central front. Here, opposed by only four light cavalry divisions, the *Chasseurs Ardennais* and 10 hurriedly prepared infantry divisions, von Kleist's two panzer corps pushed through the Ardennes and across the Meuse. By 16 May, the spearhead had advanced as far as Vervins and Montcornet. In the centre von Kluge had pushed back Blanchard's First Army to Beaumont, and Küchler had advanced south as far as Antwerp. After crossing the Meuse, von Kleist's armour moved rapidly and captured on 18 May St Quentin, nearly halfway to the Channel from Sedan. The next day he reached Amiens and Doullens, barely 40 miles from the Channel coast and on 20 May Abbeville fell.

Rundstedt's lightning drive to the Channel split the French forces in two, and cut the British line of communications with their main base at Cherbourg. With the Belgians already back on the Lys River defending Ghent, and the collapse of the French Ninth Army threatening the British rear, on 22 May the British commander, Lord Gort, ordered the BEF to hold a line extending from south of Dunkirk to the

Above: Leibstandarte's part in the campaign in the West, 10 May to 28 July 1940. After its foray into Holland *Leibstandarte* pushed south through Belgium and into France. After the evacuation of the BEF from Dunkirk, *Leibstandarte* advanced deep into central France until the Armistice on 25 June. After the victory parade in Paris did not take place, the unit transferred to Metz awaiting its next mission. It would train there from July 1940 to February 1942.

WHAT'S IN A NAME?

As with many SS units, *Leibstandarte* went through many changes between 1933 and 1945, usually getting larger and more strongly armed. The name changes over this period were as follows:

SS-*Stabswache* Berlin	from 17/3/33
SS-*Sonderkommando* Berlin,	from end 4/33
SS-*Sonderkommando* Zossen	from 10/5/33
SS-*Sonderkommando* Jüterbog	from 8/7/33
Adolf Hitler-*Standarte*	from 3/9/33
Leibstandarte Adolf Hitler	from 9/11/33
Leibstandarte-SS Adolf Hitler	from 13/4/34
Infantry Regiment (mot) LSSAH	from 24/8/39
SS-Division LSSAH	from 9/5/41
SS-Panzergrenadier Division LSSAH	from 24/11/42
1. SS-Panzer-Division LSSAH	from 22/10/43

vicinity of Arras (the canal line), in an attempt to stop a rush northward by the German forces. The only hope appeared to be an attempt to cut the German line of communications, thereby establishing a firm position from the Somme to the Scheldt. Gort attempted to drive southwards from Arras to cut the head of the advance, but promised French support failed to materialise and the attack failed in the face of determined resistance by German units. The next day the French Army finally counter-attacked with two divisions from the salient it held southeast of Lille, but this too failed. Now trapped in a pocket surrounding Dunkirk, its only remaining port, pressed by Army Group A from the south along the fragile canal line and the east by Army Group B through Belgium, where the Belgians appeared on the brink of collapse, the BEF position had become untenable.

After the battles in Holland, *Leibstandarte* was afforded a brief interlude, during which it remained under the command of Eighteenth Army. Subsequently, it was transported south, and on 20 May, crossed into France, where it transferred to XXXXIV Corps of Sixth Army, Army Group B. On 22 May, the French forces trapped in the east attempted to break out of the German trap and *Leibstandarte* was rushed into the line to stem these attacks. It was then moved into position on the Aa canal, part of the defensive perimeter around the trapped Allied forces, waiting for rescue from Britain.

That afternoon, Hitler ordered a halt in the advance, persuaded by Göring's assurances that his Luftwaffe would destroy the enemy on the beaches. However, by the time the order reached the front, the *Verfügungs* Division was already attacking the British perimeter. In response to instructions from Guderian, to whose Panzer Corps *Leibstandarte* was subordinated, the regiment was preparing to assault at Wattan. On 25 May, disregarding Hitler's orders, Dietrich ordered Jochen Peiper to

Below: The Blitzkrieg in the West was a resounding success for the German forces. Soldiers of the Waffen-SS receive the Iron Cross, 2nd Class.

lead the assault across the Aa Canal, and eliminate the British artillery positions on the Wattenberg heights, which commanded the surrounding flatlands. Guderian appeared at Dietrich's command HQ during the middle of the attack demanding to know why orders were being disobeyed, but suitably appraised of the situation and encouraged by the early successes, gave his approval and brought up the armour of the 2nd Panzer Division in support, and the bridgehead was secured.

The next day, 26 May, the British government authorised Lord Gort to begin evacuating the BEF from Dunkirk, and the following night the BEF began withdrawing to a shallow perimeter around the port. During the retreat, they were doggedly pursued by German troops. *Leibstandarte*'s 2nd Battalion,

Above: Junior NCOs of the Waffen-SS, all of whom have just received the Iron Cross, 2nd Class for their part in the campaign in the West.

tasked with capturing the key town of Wormhoudt, encountered stubborn resistance from men of the British 48th Division, and on 28 May the town was still in British hands. As fighting continued, a number of the 4th Cheshire Regiment were captured and herded into a barn, which was then raked with fire. Grenades were tossed in, and by the time an officer had halted the slaughter, 65 of the 80 POWs were dead. Those who did survive implicated Wilhelm Mohnke as the officer who gave the execution order — not the last such crime in which this fervent Nazi would be implicated. Dietrich, however, was cleared of any involvement in the war crime, as he claimed to have spent the entire day pinned down in a ditch after troops of the British Gloucestershire Regiment shot up his staff car around Esquelbecq. The incident has been the subject of controversy and numerous attempts to bring the perpetrators to justice, and remains a dark stain on *Leibstandarte* history.

With the BEF evacuation underway, and its destruction entrusted to the Luftwaffe, attention turned to the south, where the French held a line stretching along the Somme and Aisne rivers. This hastily constructed 'Weygand Line' was badly compromised by the fact that during its advance to the Channel the German forces had captured vital bridgeheads on the Somme. *Leibstandarte* and SS-*Verfügungs* Division, hastily reinforced and briefly rested after the action around Dunkirk, were attached to von Kleist's armoured group for an advance from the northwest on Paris by Bock's Army Group B.

Attacks on the Weygand Line began on 5 June, with *Leibstandarte* advancing across the Somme south of Amiens. Along the Aisne, von Rundstedt's Army Group A launched the main attack on the 9th, and with the destruction of the Oise Bridge much of von Kleist's group, including *Leibstandarte*, was rushed to the north-east into the area around Guiscard to reinforce Army Group A, capturing Laon and then Chateau-Thierry. On 11 June, despite spirited resistance, the French were forced to

Above: Young and confident. Troops of the Waffen-SS wearing their distinctive camouflage smocks and helmet covers photographed riding in an armoured troop carrier.

fall back on the Marne in deference to their open left flank, but this last line of defence was breached and on the next day four armoured divisions under Guderian broke through the line at Châlons-sur-Marne. Subsequently, Paris was declared an open city and abandoned. On 14 June Paris surrendered, but for the *Leibstandarte* the advance continued. At the spearhead of Panzer Group Kleist, it battled for crossings over the Seine, and, continuing south in pursuit of the remnants of the retreating Second and Fourth French armies, the regiment seized nearly 250 abandoned French aircraft, 4,000 men and untold other materiel at the Clermont-Ferrand aerodrome. By 17 June von Kleist was at Nevers on the Loire; to the east Guderian had reached Dijon and the Swiss border, cutting off 500,000 French troops in the Maginot Line, who were pressed from the east by Army Group C under von Leeb.

For the advance south Dietrich was placed in command of XVI Corps and tasked with attacking the rear of the French Alpine Corps, which was defending against the penetration made by the Italian Army into the French Riviera. *Leibstandarte*, whose line of advance took it west of Lyon, faced brave but ultimately futile resistance. On 22 June, the ageing Marshal Pétain called for a ceasefire, and three days later, France capitulated with armistice.

In total the campaign in France cost the *Leibstandarte* some 500 casualties. Along with the other Waffen-SS units that had fought in Poland, it had performed well in battle, and for this it was amply rewarded. During July, with the regiment quartered at the German city of Metz on the reserve of Army Group C, George Keppler, Paul Hausser and Sepp Dietrich received the Knight's Cross at the Führer's victory celebration in the Reichstag, Berlin, and on 7 September, at a ceremony at Fort Alvensleben in Metz, Himmler presented a revised colour standard to the regiment.

Although the army remained sceptical of SS discipline, in light of fresh instances of SS brutality against French colonial troops and other 'racial inferiors', Hitler now had no misgivings about expanding the SS further. In August *Leibstandarte* was upgraded to brigade status and began amphibious training for Operation *Sealöwe* — the proposed invasion of Britain. For this it was attached to XXXXV Corps, First Army, Army Group C, and in September to XXV Corps. But on 13 October, having failed to defeat the RAF over Britain, Hitler was forced to postpone *Sealöwe*. In December *Leibstandarte* transferred to LX Corps, Army Group D.

YUGOSLAVIA AND GREECE

In the spring of 1941, events in the Balkans conspired to bring about the invasion of Yugoslavia and Greece by German forces. Mussolini, hungry to emulate German successes in northern Europe, launched a disastrous and humiliating invasion of Greece on 28 October 1940, but solid defence by the Greek armies and counter-attacks launched in the new year soon had the Italian armies on the back foot. The events underlined the instability of the region, and convinced Hitler of the need to stabilise his southern flank prior to the invasion of Russia, and equally importantly, protect the vital Romanian oilfields.

In February 1941, in response to the crisis in the Balkans, *Leibstandarte* transferred from Metz to Campalung in Romania, under XIV Corps, Twelfth Army (List), in preparation for the upcoming campaign — codenamed Operation 'Marita'. Then, in March, a coup d'état in Yugoslavia against the pro-Axis regent installed a new government with an anti-German stance, blocking German access to the Greek border. Hitler now prepared another operation against Yugoslavia, codenamed 'Strafe', to run concurrent with the attack on Greece. *Leibstandarte* moved again to Temesvar, Bulgaria, where it joined *Grossdeutschland* Division and *Hermann Göring* Brigade, XXXX Corps, Twelfth Army, which was to conduct the campaign in Greece while the Second Army (Weichs), von Kleist's First Panzer Group and the Hungarian Third Army moved on Yugoslavia.

Generalfeldmarschall Wilhelm List's Twelfth Army numbered eight infantry divisions and two tank divisions, the 2nd and 9th Panzer Divisions. They were faced by troops of the British Expeditionary Force under British General Henry Maitland Wilson, that held a short line facing north-eastward along the Vermion Mountains and lower Aliakmon River, between the Greek forces holding the front in Albania and those in the Metaxas Line covering the Bulgarian border. The BEF comprised some 75,000 men, including the 6th Australian Infantry Division, the 2nd New Zealand Division and the 1st Armoured Brigade, and could field some 100 tanks. The Australian 7th Division and a Polish brigade were intended for Greece as well, but were held back for North Africa, as Rommel was at that time advancing into Cyrenaica.

The German Second Army under Maximilian von Weichs thrust south into Yugoslavia from Austria at 05:15hrs on 6 April, while von Kleist's First Panzer Group pushed towards Belgrade from Bulgaria and the Twelfth Army attacked Thrace, sending XXXX Corps westwards through the Vardar region toward Macedonia and

Above: Motorised Waffen-SS infantry supported by an anti-tank gun.

Left: SS-Obergruppenführer Sepp Dietrich discussing strategy with German Army Gebirgsjäger officers during the Greek campaign, 1 May 1941. He is accompanied by his Adjutant, Max Wunsche.

the Monastir Gap. *Leibstandarte* advanced into Yugoslavia with the 9th Panzer Division from the border town of Kustendil, heading toward Skopje in the southern Yugoslavia on the northern arm of the two-pronged advance. On 7 April the Kriva Pass and Skopje were taken after heavy fighting with the Yugoslav Third Army and *Leibstandarte* turned south, heading for the strategically important Monastir Gap, the gateway into Greece. On the open flank of the British line along the Vermion mountains and the Greek front in Albania, Monastir was taken only three days after crossing the Bulgarian border, and List's Twelfth Army, having pierced the Metaxas Line, took Salonika on the 9th, cutting off eastern Thrace and the Greek Second Army.

As it advanced to the border, the Brigade's Reconnaissance Battalion, under SS-Sturmbannführer Kurt 'Panzer' Meyer, was divided, one element forging ahead to reconnoitre the Monastir Gap and the other to skirting round the northern shore of Lake Preapa to link up with Italian forces to the west. On 10 April the *Leibstandarte* attacked through the Klidi Pass on the border with Greece and the next day won it from ANZAC troops. The British immediately began to withdraw to a temporary defensive line west of Mount Olympus, and the Greek First Army began to pull back from Albania.

Meyer's battalion was then ordered to advance through the Klissura Pass and on to Lake Kastoria. In his postwar memoirs Meyer recalled an incident during the assault when, pinned down by enemy gunfire, his soldiers could only be motivated to attack the heavily defended Allied positions when Meyer tossed a grenade at their feet! The pass was duly taken from its ANZAC defenders, and with it secured, Meyer's battalion moved on, taking Kastoria on 15 April.

On the 20th, at the Katara Pass, entrance to Epirus through the Pindus Mountains, Dietrich accepted the surrender of 16 Greek divisions from General Tsolakoglous, signalling that Greece was lost, and forcing the British and Imperial forces to begin withdrawing to the Thermopylae Line. The Metsovan Pass fell on 21 April, cutting the Greek First Army's route of escape from the area around and north of Ionnina. Three days later what remained of the Greek Army surrendered. Hounded through the Pindus and down the Aegean coast to Athens by the Luftwaffe and the pursuing *Leibstandarte*, by 25 April the British had retreated into small beachhead at Kalamata, and were evacuating towards Crete and Egypt. Having taken Patros, *Leibstandarte* crossed the Gulf of

Below: *Leibstandarte*'s campaign in the Balkans, 4 March to 30 April 1941. In a brilliant campaign the British were pushed out of Greece with great loss of life as the German forces secured their southern flank before the attack on Russia. *Leibstandarte* played a major part in the campaign.

SENIOR PERSONNEL OF *MOTORISIERTE BRIGADE DER SS-LEIBSTANDARTE ADOLF HITLER* SPRING 1941

CO Sepp Dietrich
Staff
Ia SS-Stubaf Keilnaus
Ib SS-Stubaf Ewert
IIa SS-Hstuf Max Wunsche
III SS-Stubaf Knote
IVa SS-Stubaf Bludeau
Band

1st Infantry Battalion (mot)
CO SS-Stubaf Fritz Witt
1st Company SS-Ostuf Gerd Pleib
2nd Company SS-Hstuf Schulze
3rd Company SS-Hstuf Shiller
4th Company (MG) SS-Hstuf Krocza
5th Company (Hy) SS-Hstuf Grob

2nd Infantry Battalion (mot)
CO SS-Stubaf Theodor Wisch
6th Company
7th Company SS-Hstuf Rudolf Sandig
8th Company SS-Ostuf Beutin
9th Company (MG) SS-Hstuf Wielk
10th Company (Hy) SS-Hstuf Scappini

3rd Infantry Battalion (mot)
CO SS-Stubaf Weidenhaupt
11th Company SS-Hstuf Frey
12th Company SS-Hstuf Hubert Meyer
13th Company SS-Hstuf Hempel
14th Company (MG) SS-Hstuf Max
  Hansen
15th Company (Hy) SS-Ostuf Olboeter

IV Infantry Battalion (mot)
  (from 10 June 1941)
CO SS-Sturmbannführer Jahnke
16th Company SS-Hstuf Klingemeyer
17th Company SS-Ostuf Wandt
18th Company SS-Hstuf Kling
19th Company SS-Hstuf Meiforth
20th Company SS-Hstuf Kolitz

Guard Battalion
at Berlin-Lichterfelde

Artillery Regiment (mot)
CO SS-Staf.

1st Group CO—SS-Stubaf Sukkau
  1st Battery SS-Hstuf Teufel
  2nd Battery SS-Hstuf Cischek
  3rd Battery SS-Ostuf Horns

2nd Group CO—SS-Stubaf Mertsch
  4th Battery (hy) SS-Hstuf Schroder
  5th Battery (hy) SS-Ostuf Heberer
  6th Battery SS-Hstuf Fend
  7th Battery SS-Ostuf Dr Naumann
  8th Battery SS-Hstuf Urbanitz

SS-Pionier Battalion (mot)
CO SS-Stubaf Christian Hansen
1st Company SS-Hstuf Anhalt
2nd Company SS-Hstuf Wendler
3rd Company SS-Ostuf Tscholtsch

Signals Battalion (mot)
CO SS-Ostubaf Keilhaus

Support Column (mot)
CO SS-Stubaf Bernhard Siebken

Flak Battalion
CO SS-Hstuf Bernhard Krause
1st Battery SS-Hstuf Ullerich
2nd Battery SS-Hstuf Mobius
3rd Battery SS-Hstuf Kappus

Heavy Infantry Battalion (mot)
CO SS-Stubaf Steineck
1st Company (Lt IG) SS-Ostuf Jurgensen
2nd Company (Hy IG) SS-Ostuf Wiest
3nd Company (PzJg) SS-Ostuf Woest

Reconnaissance Battalion
CO SS-Stubaf Kurt Meyer
1st Company (MC) SS-Ostuf G. Bremer
2nd Company (MC) SS-Hstuf Hugo Kraas
3rd Company (Lt AC) SS-Ostuf Bottcher
4th Company (Hy) Nachrichtenzug

Sturmgeschütz Battalion
CO SS-Stubaf Schönberger
1st Battery SS-Hstuf Wiesemann
2nd Battery SS-Hstuf Prinz

Abbreviations
Ostuf   Obersturmführer
Hstuf   Hauptsturmführer
Stubaf   Sturmbannführer
Ostubaf Obersturmbannführer

Above: German troops being greeted with obvious enthusiasm by Greek women, some of whom are giving the 'German Greeting' — the 'Heil Hitler' salute — May 1941.

Corinth into southern Greece in pursuit of the BEF, but through a skillfully executed withdrawal the bulk of the British forces were evacuated by sea.

On 27 April *Leibstandarte* was at Pirgus, and the following day the remaining British troops in Greece surrendered. In all the Greek campaign cost the British some 12,000 men killed, wounded or captured, most of them in the final desperate defensive battles around the evacuation ports. The cost to *Leibstandarte* was 93 killed, 225 wounded and three missing, and it was afforded a few days' rest. On 8 May the victorious German Army paraded through Athens, where the passing motorcyclists were handed flowers from cheering Greeks.

In Yugoslavia, Wehrmacht forces took a mere 12 days to bring Yugoslavia under heel. By 13 April German motorised and armoured elements had linked up in Belgrade, and on the 15th, Sarajevo was occupied. Finally, on the 17th, the Yugoslavs formally surrendered. Some 6,000 officers and 338,000 NCOs and men became prisoners of war, although the larger part managed to escape and form an army of partisans around Tito.

OCCUPATION DUTY — CZECHOSLOVAKIA

After the Balkan diversion, *Leibstandarte* was transferred back to Prague, Czechoslovakia, for rest and refitting in preparation for the delayed invasion of the Soviet Union. At this time it was upgraded to divisional status, becoming *1. SS-Motorisierte Division Leibstandarte Adolf Hitler* (1st SS-Motorised Division *LAH*), but even with the addition of a motorised infantry battalion and other reinforcements, strength stood at only 10,796, half that of the *Das Reich*, *Totenkopf* and *Wiking* divisions. The shortfall was due to a manpower shortage that was already beginning to manifest itself at home. The Wehrmacht had placed restrictions

Above: Troops of the advance guard from *Leibstandarte* after crossing the Gulf of Corinth, 27 April 1941.

Left: Waffen-SS troops were also employed on duties other than fighting. Here a guard examines the pass books of new recruits about the join the Waffen-SS. Recruitment into the SS was not as straightforward as Himmler or Hitler would have liked, because the regular army was reluctant to let go men from its manpower pool. The SS was forced to look elsewhere — initially at the police force and then outside Germany, mainly at 'ethnic Germans' or those with 'Nordic blood'. Himmler certainly wanted to expand the organisation internationally and of the 39 SS divisions set up between 1933 and 1945, eight were fully or partially composed of 'ethnic Germans', and 19 of other nationalities, including Yugoslavs, Dutch, Italians, Belgians, French, Scandinavians, Ukrainians, Russians, men from the Baltic states and Hungarians.

WAFFEN-SS UNIT STRENGTHS ON 22 JUNE 1941 FOR OPERATION 'BARBAROSSA'	
1st SS Division	10,796
2nd SS Division	19,021
3rd SS Division	18,754
4th SS Division	17,347
5th SS Division	19,377
6th SS Division	10,573
Himmler's Command Staff	18,438
Administrative	4,007
Reserve	29,809
Concentration Camp Inspectorate	7,200
SS Guard Battalions	2,159
Garrison posts	992
Officer/NCO schools	1,028
SS Volunteer Battalion Nordost	904
TOTAL	160,405

on the number of men it would permit to join the Waffen-SS, and so Reichsführer Himmler began to fill the ranks of the SS with increasing numbers of *Volksdeutsche* from the occupied territories. However, *Leibstandarte* remained a unique exception to this new policy, as Himmler was determined that it should remain 'racially pure'. For the time being its exclusive entry standards were maintained.

RUSSIA — OPERATION 'BARBAROSSA'

As the French campaign drew to its conclusion, Hitler began to feel that an attack on the Soviet Union was the best means of achieving two important strategic aims. Firstly, by denying Britain a potential ally, he could force its people to accept negotiated peace. Secondly, it presented an opportunity to satisfy a fundamental ambition of Nazism — the acquisition of territory to extend its living space (*Lebensraum*). Equally importantly, he had an inherent hatred for Bolshevism, was contemptuous of Slavic peoples and mistrusted the Soviet Union's ambitions in Europe. Thus even before the fall of France, the OKH was planning for an invasion of Soviet soil, and this gathered increasing impetus as hopes for a swift victory over Britain diminished.

For 'Barbarossa', some 3,350 tanks in four Panzer armies were available, in addition to 3,050,000 men, another 750,000 from Finland and Romania, 7,184 artillery pieces, and 600,000 motor vehicles, with support from over 3,000 aircraft. The ground forces were organised into three army groups under three newly promoted field marshals — Wilhelm Ritter von Leeb had the north, Fedor von Bock the centre and Gerd von Rundstedt the south. All of them agreed that the war hinged on the use of the Panzer armies, acting independently ahead of the infantry, but for the start of the Russian campaign, they were to be in close cooperation with the infantry in battles of encirclement that aimed at netting the Soviet forces before they could retreat behind the safety of the River Dnieper

German Army estimates, which were approximately correct, placed the total initial strength of the Soviet forces at 203 divisions and 46 motorised or armoured brigades. Of these 33 divisions and five brigades were in the east, leaving about 2,300,000 men to meet the European invasion. The Soviet air forces were numerically twice as strong as the Germans, but mostly equipped with obsolete types. Russia had 10,000 tanks, including a few of the excellent T-34 that was not yet in full production. The T-34s that did see action had a sobering effect on the Germans, leading to an immediate re-evaluation of the PzKpfw III and IV, the mainstays of the *Panzerwaffe*. The reaction to the T-34 would be the PzKpfw V Panther, the best medium tank of the war. The other surprise to soldiers who had been taught that the Slavs were subhuman was the determination and tenacity of the ordinary troops. An example of this was seen at the citadel of Brest-Litovsk where individual soldiers resisted for weeks after the main strongpoint had fallen. In fact, the real weakness of the Soviet forces was its officer corps, within which almost none of those who had survived the brutal purges of the 1930s had military competence or experience. This weakness was first exposed during the 1940-41 Winter War with Finland, and was again during 'Barbarossa'.

Badly delayed by excursions in the Balkans and complicated reorganisation and refitting, on 22 June 'Barbarossa' was finally unleashed on a 1,800-mile front against the Soviet Union. The Red Army was totally unprepared to meet the onslaught, and the seven divisions opposing von Leeb in the Baltic states were rapidly swept aside. By the end of the month, having destroyed an estimated 15 Soviet divisions, the

Right: Troops from LSSAH drive through a village somewhere in the east. The reaction towards the advancing Germans was mixed. In most areas they were treated as invaders but in areas that had felt the worst effects of the Soviet purges, the Germans were welcomed.

ORGANISATION OF *1. SS-MOTORISIERTE DIVISION LEIBSTANDARTE ADOLF HITLER* IN MAY 1941

Divisional HQ, HQ Staff and Band

4 x Infantry Battalions
  Staff
  3 x Inf Companies
  1 x MG Company
  1 x Hy Company
    of 2 x A/tk Platoons, 1 x Mortar
    Platoon, 1 x Pionier Platoon

1 x Heavy Weapons Battalion
  (created 10 June 1941)
  Staff
  1 x Lt Inf Gun Company (75mm)
  1 x Hy Inf Gun Company (150mm)
  1 x A/tk Company (47mm)
  1 x Field Gun Company (75mm)
  1 x AA Company (37mm)

Guard Battalion (4 x Companies
  at Lichterfelde Kaserne)

1 x Artillery Regiment
  Staff
  1 x Battalion (3 x 150mm btys)
  1 x Battalion (2 x 150mm, 1 x 88mm)
  1 x Lt Arty Column

1 x Reconnaissance Battalion
  2 x MC Companies
  1 x AC Company
  1 x Hy AC Company
  1 x Sig Platoon

1 x AA Battalion
  2 x 3.7cm Batteries
  1 x 2cm Battery

1 x Pionier Battalion
  Staff
  3 x Companies
  1 x Bridging Column
  1 x Lt Pionier Column

Sturmgeschütz Battalion
  (Abteilung Schönberger)
  1 x StuG Battery
  1 x PzJg (4.7 cm) Company

1 x Signals Battalion
  1 x Telephone Company
  1 x Wireless Company

Supply Services
  Staff
  1 x Workshop Company
  1 x Weapons Workshop Platoon
  2 x Fuel Columns
  6 x Motorised Columns
  1 x Bakery Company
  1 x Butchery Company
  1 x Rations Office
  1 x Field Post Office

Medical Services
  2 x Medical Companies
  1 x Field Hospital
  1 x Ambulance Platoon
  1 x Surgery

Left: Waffen-SS troops manning a mortar in the tundra somewhere on the Finnish-Russian border. It's likely to be the 8.1cm GrW34 (GrW= *Granatewerfer* =mortar) that proved better than the smaller 5cm light mortar (GrW36). Experience on the Russian fronts led to the development of a 12cm mortar (the heavy GrW42) often on a two-wheel trolley, and German troops made use of captured Russian heavy mortars whenever they could.

Below: German troops closing the ring around the Soviets holding out in Kiev.

Right: Waffen-SS troops proudly display a captured Communist banner.

Inset: Large numbers of Russians were taken prisoner in the early stages of 'Barbarossa'. Here, prisoners, stripped of their arms, equipment and helmets, are made to stand with their arms raised. The woman prisoner in the front row is presumed to be a female commissar.

Below right: A reconnaissance detachment from a Waffen-SS unit holds a meeting in open ground from the back of a four-wheeled armoured car — probably an SdKfz 261 with frame antenna in raised position.

Army Group North drew up on the western Dvina River. Meanwhile, Bock's Army Group Centre crossed the border on 27/28 June in the wake of 7th Panzer Division, and advanced on the northern fringes of the impassable Pripet Marches, moving toward its main objective — Moscow. At Bialystock it encircled a vast army and again at Minsk another large encirclement yielded more than 150,000 Soviet prisoners.

During the initial attack *Leibstandarte* was undergoing reorganisation into a division as part of the reserve of the First Panzer Army, Army Group South (Rundstedt) in the Lublin area, and as such took no part. It moved on to Ostorwiecz and finally, a week after the invasion, crossed the Vistula and headed into the western Ukraine, entering the battle attached to von Mackensen's III Panzer Corps, itself part of von Kleist's First Panzer Army, and which included the SS *Wiking* Division and the 13th and 14th Panzer Divisions.

Initially Army Group South (Sixth, Eleventh and Seventeenth Armies), which was tasked with cutting off and destroying Soviet forces west of the Dnieper River, 300 miles into southern Russia, made stunning progress. The line of advance took it along the main road to Kiev, a major objective on the route towards the grand prize, Rostov. Such was the pace of the advance that the infantry began to be left behind, inviting attacks on the vulnerable German flanks; furthermore, the Russian forces of the Kiev Military District under General Kiroponos were sited in better-prepared defences than on the north and central fronts. In this situation, *Leibstandarte* was again able to demonstrate the advantages of motorised infantry by filling the widening gap between the armoured spearhead and the slower (largely horse-drawn or pedestrian) infantry. In one instance 73rd Panzer Division met with unexpectedly fierce counter-attacks by Russian armour at Dubno and Olyka; *Leibstandarte* was rushed in to support, and although the ensuing battle cost 683 killed and wounded, it prevented the Soviets from cutting the lengthening line of communications.

Consistent with the conventional military doctrine at that time, which emphasised defence, a fortified line running from the Gulf of Finland to the Black Sea was built in western Russia during the 1930s. Behind this the Russian forces of the Southern Front retreated, while launching fierce counter-attacks against von Kleist's armour, which was advancing on the left flank at an average rate of 20 miles a day. On 3 July Stalin announced that the Soviet government would welcome aid from the west and called for a scorched earth policy, which would leave the invaders with 'not a kilogram of grain or a litre of gasoline', while rallying the populace to the defence of the motherland.

The Stalin Line, despite its innumerable obstacles, proved too weak to hold the German armour. Von Kleist broke through east of Zhitomir at Miropol on 8 July, driving a wedge between the two Soviet armies. Moving quickly on the main road to Kiev, *Leibstandarte* ran into strong enemy forces north of Romanovka. At the same time the renamed Southwest Front under General Budenny launched a concerted Soviet counter-attack along the whole of the south-western front and the brigade was temporarily forced onto the back foot, defending the prizes it had won during the advance. But the huge losses incurred by the Soviet forces soon brought a respite in the attacks and *Leibstandarte* was soon on the attack again. Shepetovka was taken and then, in support of the 13th Panzer, Zhitomir itself.

Although von Rundstedt now stood poised to take Kiev, Hitler paused to contemplate a move on Uman, a major transport hub for the Crimea. Such a move had the added attraction of encircling the Soviet forces holding up the Seventeenth and Eleventh Armies in the centre and on the right flank. In the event his hand was forced. Budenny began advancing a section of his forces on Odessa, leaving the

Below: Mosquitoes and flies could prove to be an unbearable nuisance during the summer season on certain sectors of the Eastern Front. As a form of protection this Untersturmführer has covered his head with a mosquito net.

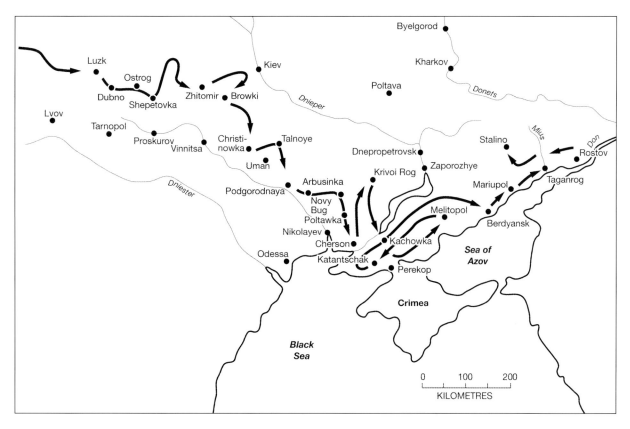

Above: The Russian campaign — *Leibstandarte* in the Ukraine, 2 July 1941 to 26 July 1942.

remainder in defence of Uman, and the German Sixth Army was ordered to move south-east from in front of Kiev on the left flank of Army Group South. *Leibstandarte* was again instrumental in preventing Soviet counter-thrusts from piercing the flanks of von Kleist's armoured column, spearheading the advance. Taking the cities of Novo Ukraina and Kirovograd on 25 and 30 July, the Sixth Army met the Seventeenth Army (Manteuffel and Schobert) on the Southern Bug River some 50 miles east of Uman on 8 August, trapping two whole Soviet armies and a large part of another. In an attempt to break the encirclement, the Soviets threw armour, cavalry and scores of infantrymen into the battle, and for its part in defeating these relentless attacks *Leibstandarte* earned considerable praise from corps commander, Generalmajor Werner Kempf.

Soviet forces in the Uman pocket were finally eliminated on 22 August, but the focus of the advance had already switched to the industrial centre of Cherson, north-east of Odessa. After bitter fighting *Leibstandarte* took Bubry and subsequently the road junction at Sasselje. Arriving at Cherson on 17 August, *Leibstandarte* fought through the streets for three days before the defenders finally abandoned the city.

During the march south another atrocity had allegedly taken place. According to a postwar account of a Waffen-SS journalist serving with the 4th Battalion, east of Gejgova, men from the battalion found the mutilated bodies of six fellow SS troopers who had been previously captured and executed in the town's NKVD headquarters. In reprisal, Dietrich ordered *Leibstandarte* to shoot all surrendering Soviet troops for three days, and in the ensuing slaughter an estimated 4,000 were killed. For want of reliable evidence, the allegations remained unproven.

Above: A command post somewhere on the Eastern Front.

Left: Destroying enemy armour is thirsty work. Men of the Waffen-SS, one from the *Totenkopf* Division, take a pause to drink from a field flask with a burning tank behind them, 18 August 1944. Note the tank destruction badge on the right sleeve of the soldier drinking.

Opposite, Above: The encirclement battle of Uman. Ready for action in their camouflaged smocks and helmet covers these Waffen-SS gunners start firing their 75mm LG18 light infantry gun at the Soviet stronghold, 3 September 1941.

Opposite, Below: The defence of Breslau near to the Czech border. Roadblocks were set up to deny or slow down the enemy advance. Men of a Waffen-SS unit prepare an anti-tank rifle.

KIEV AND THE UKRAINE

Above: The division's chief medical officer examining the wound of a young SS-Grenadier (note the *Leibstandarte* cuff title). The 1941 battles in Russia decimated the brigade, which lost — as did the whole of the German forces — many of its most experienced NCOs and young officers. By early 1942, while still on the offensive the writing was on the wall: Russian numbers would ensure that the German forces would lose a battle of attrition. Altogether, by early 1942 *Leibstandarte*'s initial complement of 10,796 had suffered 5,281 casualties.

By mid-August the first, highly successful, phase of the campaign against the Soviet Union was nearly ended. Fighting on the Central Front had been characterised by rapid advances across the flat empty steppes of central Russia as far as the area south of Smolensk, against sporadic and limited resistance. The capture of Smolensk on 7 August brought 850,000 Russian captives, and towards the end of the month the ferocious fighting in the vicinity of Vaskovo-Chochlovka-Rudnaya began to slacken off. Army Group Centre was then moved into defensive positions to hold the salient that had been put into the Soviet line west of Yelnya by the 360-mile wide advance.

The OKH now felt that the maximum effort should be directed against Moscow, but Hitler was unconvinced of the strategic value of this target. Encouraged by confident predictions that the war was already won, he decided to redirect some of Army Group Centre to the south to take the Crimea and the Donets Basin industrial region thus cutting the Russians off from the oilfields of the Caucasus. He also looked north with a view to taking Leningrad. He was insistent that only after Leningrad had been secured, and Army Group South had made significant inroads, would the advance on Moscow resume.

Acting on these orders, on 25 August the Second Army and the Second Panzer Army turned southward from the Army Group Centre flank. The advance was slowed by rain and mud but the defences of the Soviet Army were breached on 12 September, and on 16 September the lead elements of the Second Army and the First Army, which had moved northward from the Dnieper bend, met 150 miles east of Kiev. Denied permission to withdraw by Stalin, the seven Soviet armies inside the Kiev pocket surrendered on the 19th after five days of resistance. In addition to those lost at Uman in the south, this amounted to nearly 1.5 million men — or half of the current active strength of the Soviet army.

After the battle of Uman, *Leibstandarte* was placed on the reserve of XXXXVIII Corps, First Panzer Group, Eleventh Army, for a much-needed period of rest. It was soon on the advance south again, now under command of the XXX Corps, Eleventh Army (von Manstein), into the dry, dusty steppes of the Nogai Steppe. On 6 September, Hitler had another change of heart and decided that operations against Moscow would resume, and reinforced Army Group Centre with elements of Army Group South. On 6 October, after a fateful delay, it returned to action in front of Moscow.

In the Ukraine, having advanced as far south as the Black Sea, *Leibstandarte* turned east toward Rostov on the River Don. Capturing Romanovka, at Melitopol the brigade was met by a fierce Soviet counter-attack, which broke the sector of the line held by the Third Romanian Army and threatened an envelopment. *Leibstandarte* was again rushed into the line to beat back the attackers, and subsequently took Berdyansk on the Sea of Azov. Moving along the north shore of the lake, it took Taganrog, where according to some accounts, troops executed Soviet prisoners on Dietrich's orders as a reprisal for the brutal execution of SS men by the district NKVD. On 20 October von Manstein's exhausted forces attacked the five-mile wide Perekop Isthmus, guarding the gateway to the Crimea, and 10 days later broke through and poured onto the peninsula, aiming toward Kerch and Sevastopol.

Even after this most dramatic advance the sheer numerical superiority of the Red Army, the vastness of the terrain and the coming of winter rains that turned the roads into quagmires began to make a quick victory increasingly improbable. Army Group Centre's attacks stopped dead in their tracks on the heavily defences of

Moscow, despite the fact that the troops were fighting in the capital itself, and in the south the advance on Rostov began to bog down.

On 15 November Army Group South reached the Don River, the last natural obstacle before Stalingrad. It had penetrated some 600 miles into Russian territory, in five months of bitter fighting. *Leibstandarte* was transferred to the command of III Corps, First Panzer Army, and on the 17th began the attack on Rostov on the Don from the Black Sea coast. The 3rd Company assaulted across the main railway bridge and captured it intact, earning SS-Hauptsturmführer Heinrich Springer the Knight's Cross. Kleist's armour poured over this vital crossing and on 21 November took the city. For *Leibstandarte* came the prize of 10,000 prisoners, 159 artillery pieces, 56 tanks and two armoured trains.

It was a brief victory. During the following week the army, racked by sickness, badly overstretched and plagued by shortages, was battered by a fierce counter-offensive by Timoshenko's Ninth and Thirty-seventh Armies, and although retreat from Rostov was soon the only viable option, Hitler refused to countenance any such move. Responding to Hitler's 'no retreat' order of 30 November, von Rundstedt stated, '. . . it is madness attempting to hold. In the first place the troops cannot do it, and in the second place if they do not retreat they will be destroyed. I repeat that this order be rescinded or find someone else.' Hitler sent back a message that same night, telling him to give up his command. He was replaced by Walther von Reichenau.

Defeat at Rostov exposed how badly overstretched the German forces were and the inherent flaws in Hitler's decision to halt the advance on Moscow. The battles in Rostov left *Leibstandarte* decimated. At the end of November it was pulled out

Above: Among all the signs of a fierce firefight — empty cartridge boxes and shell cases strewn around them — these men of a Waffen-SS infantry unit pause after repelling an enemy assault. During the first winter in Russia temperatures fell as low as -40°C: even the best winter clothing — and there wasn't much of that available — could not protect men and machines and thousands suffered from the extreme conditions. A new winter uniform was designed and available for the next winter, 1942–43, but it had one drawback: it was used so frequently that it got dirty. Too heavy to wash comfortably, the easiest solution was to wear white overalls or snow suits over the top.

and spent December in defensive positions outside Rostov behind the Mius. Here during the first winter of the Russian campaign, it engaged in defensive battles in temperatures that sank as low as −40°C. A deep carpet of snow made movement almost impossible, and partisan actions ensured that little or nothing in the way of supplies got through. During this time the daily food ration fell to only 150 grams. For the troops, the troubles were heightened by Hitler's ban on the distribution of winter clothing, which he reasoned would be detrimental to morale.

Within the ranks of *Leibstandarte*, Dietrich devolved command to the independent unit commanders, which no doubt saved the *Leibstandarte* further casualties. But even in these straits, the unit earned plaudits. In a Christmas communique with Himmler, III Panzer Corps Commander General Eberhard von Mackensen wrote: '. . . Every unit wants to have the *Leibstandarte* as its adjacent unit. The unit's internal discipline, its refreshing eagerness, its cheerful enthusiasm, its unshakable calmness in a crisis and its toughness are examples to us all . . . This truly is an elite unit.'

For the coming year prospects on the Eastern Front were bleak. The combat experience of the early Blitzkrieg years had been lost on the steppes of Russia through battle and weather casualties. And the new year promised a different Soviet Army, one now supplied with better tanks, guns and aircraft, and supplies from the US and United Kingdom. Furthermore, behind the German lines partisan forces were becoming a serious threat to the overstretched supply lines, which crossed hundreds of miles of overrun but not conquered territory.

At the beginning of 1942 *Leibstandarte* was firmly entrenched in positions outside Rostov, in anticipation of an expected Soviet offensive. At this time a Panzer Battalion was added to the order of battle. It was comprised of three companies equipped with PzKpfw IIIs and IVs.

In February *Leibstandarte* was transferred to the command of XIV Corps in the Mius area, and for the remainder of the winter, sub-zero temperatures rendered movement next to impossible as the brigade fought containing actions against

Below: The victors of Kharkov. Troops from the *Leibstandarte-SS Adolf Hitler, Das Reich and Totenkopf* divisions, all of whom took part in the battle for Kharkov, being congratulated by Reichsminister Dr Goebbels in his Berlin residence, 1 April 1943.

limited Soviet actions in the Mius and Donets area. As the first winter in Russia drew to a close, 5,281 men of the *Leibstandarte* had lost their lives in Russia.

In Berlin, recriminations for the failure of the Moscow campaign saw 35 leading generals, including all of the army group leaders and Guderian and Höpner, dismissed. Hitler appointed himself as direct Commander-in-Chief of the Army, and during the spring assumed the role of commander-in-chief for all operations on the Eastern Front from his headquarters at Rastenburg (the *Wolfschanze* or Wolf's Lair). Here he outlined his plans for the summer operations. He ordained that these would be limited to a full-scale offensive in the south, towards the Don River, Stalingrad and the Caucasus oilfields, the capture of which he saw as the decisive stroke. Not only would this cut the Soviets off from their fuel, but also achieve an even more important objective, namely the 'final destruction of the Soviet Union's remaining human defensive strength.' Hitler's plan was for a series of successive converging attacks; the first phase was to be an enveloping thrust on the Kursk–Voronezh line, which would carry the German front to the Don River. Then the attack would proceed to Stalingrad and across the Kerch Strait to the Taman Peninsula.

The Soviet High Command, which had also planned to take the initiative when the good weather returned, got their attack in first, launching a disastrous strike on the South-west Front toward Kharkov on 12 May. South-east of Kharkov the Soviet South-west Front (Timoshenko) broke through the lines near Dnepropetrovsk, where the German forces had captured a huge power plant. *Leibstandarte*, as part of III Corps, was rushed in to fill the breach in the line, and held fast in these positions until the Soviet attack was beaten off. Although initially successful, the Soviets met with strong German resistance and on 25 May a German armoured force struck into to the Izyum bridgehead, sealed off the pocket and netted 240,000 prisoners. The plans for a Soviet summer offensive collapsed at a stroke.

Above left: A Grille — a 15cm sIG33 on a PzKpfw 38 (t) chassis — supporting Waffen-SS infantry somewhere on the Eastern Front, July 1943.

Above: Camouflage comes in many forms. Here a soldier of the Waffen-SS on sentry duty has camouflaged himself with bunches of reeds held to his body by his waist belt. Presumably, he was operating in a reeded, watery area.

UNITS OF 1st SS-PANZERGRENADIER DIVISION *LEIBSTANDARTE* ADOLF HITLER AS AT NOVEMBER 1942

1st Panzergrenadier Regiment
2nd Panzergrenadier Regiment

Panzer Regiment 1 (from November 1942)
   1st Battalion (PzKpfw III, IV)
   2nd Battalion (PzKpfw III, IV)
   Panzer Workshop Company
   Panzer Pionier Company

Artillery Regiment
   1st Battalion (150mm, 88mm)
   2nd Battalion (88mm)
   3rd Battalion (88mm)

Reconnaissance Battalion
Flak Battalion
Panzerjäger Battalion
Sturmgeschütz Battalion
Pionier Battalion
Signals Platoon
Supply Troops
Workshop Company
Weapons Workshop Platoon
Bakery Company
Butchery Company
Rations Office
Field Post Office
Medical Battalion
Field Hospital

REFIT AND REDESIGNATION

A month later, on 28 June, the Second and Fourth Panzer Armies of Army Group South opened the German summer offensive. *Leibstandarte*, having been transferred to the reserve of First Panzer Army, moved in May to Stalino for an intended refit and took no part in this campaign. Subsequently, in June it returned to III Corps in the Rostov area before being pulled back to France, to meet a feared Allied invasion of Northwest Europe. Stationed in the Evreux region, west of Paris, and attached to the SS-Panzer Corps, Fifteenth Army, Army Group D, it participated in a ceremonial parade through Paris in front of Generalfeldmarschall von Rundstedt, and during the summer underwent a much needed rest and refit. The formation, which had already received a tank battalion (see page 40), was upgraded and began training as a panzergrenadier division. Significantly, due to manpower shortages, *Volksdeutsche* ('ethnic Germans' — ie people born outside Germany but, according to Nazi racial rules, of German racial descent) were for the first time allowed into the division.

In October, *Leibstandarte* moved south for a spell of occupation duty in Vichy France and also spent time in Normandy. On 22 October it was formally redesignated a panzergrenadier division, and renamed SS-Panzergrenadier Division *Leibstandarte* SS Adolf Hitler. Panzergrenadier units were required to accompany armour over difficult terrain into action, and were provided with both supportive firepower and safety against enemy fire by purpose-designed *Schützenpanzerwagen* (SPW/armoured personnel carriers). Suffice to say that although they pioneered the concept of mobile infantry warfare, Germany was never able to fully complete the formation of Panzergrenadier units, because until the very end of the war it was unable to produce enough armoured transports to equip even a fair proportion of the Panzergrenadier units. (For a detailed discussion of the development of the Panzergrenadier see the 'Spearhead' series title *2 Grossdeutschland*.)

In November *Leibstandarte* was still on occupation duty in southern (Vichy) France, as part of the reserve of Army Group D, where its armour was reorganised into two battalions in a panzer regiment. The next month two new companies were added, equipped with the new PzKpfw VI Tiger Is. At this time division strength was a nominal 678 officers, 20,166 NCOs and men, but many of these were poorly trained and inexperienced and, furthermore, at the end of December some of the veteran NCOs were transferred to form the cadre for the 9th SS-Panzer Division

A *Leibstandarte* veteran remembered: 'It was those defensive battles in Russia which I shall always remember for the sheer beauty of the fighting, rather than the victorious advances. Many of us died horribly, some even as cowards, but for those who lived . . . it was well worth all the dreadful suffering and danger. After a time we reached a point where we were not concerned for ourselves or even for Germany, but lived entirely for the next clash, the next engagement with the enemy.'

During the winter of 1942–43 the tide of the war turned against Germany, which now found itself matched on all fronts. On the Eastern Front it was contending with a enemy vastly different from the one it had attacked 18 months previously. Elsewhere, better leadership and equipment was also beginning to tell against the German armies. But in the east it was most obviously losing the war of supply and of numbers, where the Soviet Union was beginning to exhibit its vastly greater capacity to replace losses of men and materiel. Furthermore, by now the best Russian aircraft and tanks had achieved a parity with German equipment. In the coming battles the German forces, firmly on the defensive, would be tested to the limit.

On 19 November 1942, the Russians attacked the Romanian Third Army positions north of Stalingrad and destroyed its front within hours. The next day came another attack, on the Romanian corps to the south, and by 22 November the Soviet forces had met at Kalach, trapping the German Fourth Panzer Army around Stalingrad. Then, on 16 December, the Soviets rolled over the Italian Eighth Army positions on the right flank of Army Group B and thus extended their offensive west of the city. Finally, on 14 January of the new year, with nearly 300,000 Germans and Romanian troops still trapped in the pocket, the Russians moved up the Don again, this time to strike the Hungarian Second Army on the flank of Army Group B (now commanded by Maximilian von Weichs) south of Voronezh. The Hungarians collapsed, opening a 200-mile front between Voronezh and Lugansk (Voroshilovgrad). The Soviets then turned southwards to the Donets, threatening to envelop the remnants of Army Group B and Army Group Don, which was still battling to keep open Army Group A's lifeline to the west at Rostov. Ten days later they struck again at the German Second Army north of Voronezh, and in three days had encircled two of its three corps.

With Army Group South now close to collapse in the face of this renewed offensive, *Leibstandarte*, currently on OKH reserve, Army Group B, was recalled from France in mid-January and sent to reinforce the weak points in the Ukraine as part of the newly created SS Panzer Corps, under Hubert Lanz. Hitler had agreed to the formation of an SS Corps in 1942, which would allow Waffen-SS divisions to fight together as a coherent force, rather then being distributed throughout the different army groups. Lanz was ordered to hold Kharkov at all costs, and sent *Leibstandarte* into defensive positions along the River Donets, with *Das Reich* in positions to the east of the river. Although already overstretched on a 70-mile front, the division was further weakened by the deployment of Fritz Witt's Panzergrenadier regiment to defensive positions at Kupyansk, and the detachment of the 7th Battalion to the front as SS-Brigade Schuldt.

The Red Army advance ground on through January and into early February, slowly pushing back Army Group Don, and with it *Das Reich*, on to the Mius/Donets defensive line. On the flanks of the SS positions, the 320th Infantry Division crumbled in the face of a concerted Soviet assault, and in headlong retreat to the Donets with 1,500 wounded was surrounded. Led by the SS-Sturmbannführer Jochen Peiper, who was to distinguish himself on numerous future occasions, the 3rd Battalion of *Leibstandarte* made a daring penetration behind the enemy lines and extricated the division from disaster.

KHARKOV

The encirclement and destruction of Axis forces at Stalingrad in February 1943 was a catastrophe of the worst kind for Germany. With the annihilation of the Sixth Army, and the destruction of the greater part of Fourth Panzer Army, five of the seven divisions of the Romanian Third Army, and nearly the whole Sixth Romanian and Seventh Italian Armies, almost immediately a vast gap was formed in the front line, through which Russian troops stormed toward toward Rostov, Kursk and Kharkov. On 8 February Kursk fell. Not wishing to risk another encirclement, Hitler gave his permission on 6 February to withdraw Army Group Don to the line of the Mius and Donets Rivers, and in nine days this was achieved. But with the Soviet advance still

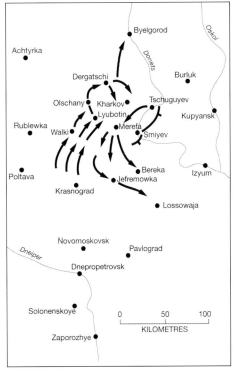

Below: *Leibstandarte* at Kharkov, 22 January–23 March 1943. One of the greatest of Erich von Manstein's victories, the recapture of Kharkov finished the Soviet 1942–43 winter offensive and, albeit at great cost, straightened the lines on the Eastern Front except for the salient at Kursk. Had the German counterattack continued, the salient may have fallen to the victorious German armies. Instead indecision let the advantage swing over to the Russians against whose defensive bulwarks the might of the German Panzers would be blunted.

Right: Men and armour — in the shape of a snow-camouflaged PzKpfw IV — from the LSSAH Division moving up to the front, March 1943.

Below right: A three-man MG34 machine gun crew operating in deep snow. The MG34 was a brilliant weapon — almost too well made, because German companies found it hard to keep manufacturing quantities high. It was, therefore, superseded by the MG42 (see caption below) although MG34s would remain in service throughout the war.

Below: Motorcycle troops preparing to move off check their ammunition and weapons. The machine gun in the foreground is an MG42, probably the best machine gun of the war. Easier to manufacture than the MG34, it was made from simple metal pressings. With a 1,200 rpm rate of fire, and a quick-release barrel change that allowed a skilled operative to do so in only a few seconds, over 750,000 MG42s were made by the end of the war.

moving at full speed, the right flank of Army Group B was forced back on to Kharkov, and on the southern front, where von Manstein had taken over command, the forces had been severely weakened by the savage fighting.

Although von Manstein did not share Hitler's views on the need for strong fixed defences and was convinced that the numerically inferior German forces could only match the Red Army by taking full advantage of their superiority mobility in a fluid defensive pattern, the Führer concluded that no more territory was to be lost, and ordered both armies to hold. Hitler, remembering the way the Waffen-SS units had defended themselves during the winter of 1941, ordered SS-Panzer Corps (under former SS-VT commander Paul Hausser) to hold Kharkov. For *Leibstandarte* Kharkov was a familiar battleground, but to contemplate defending the city in winter against Soviet forces seven times greater in numerical strength was nothing less than suicidal. On 15 February Hausser, who had no desire to preside over a second Stalingrad, ignored Hitler's orders and allowed SS-Panzer Corps to pull out of the city towards Krasnograd. There they held firm and destroyed the Soviet vanguard, bringing the Kharkov offensive to a standstill.

However, with the withdrawal, a 100-mile wide gap appeared between the right flank of Army Group B and Army Group Don, through which the six Soviet tank corps of the Popov Group struck southward and westward across the Donets, moving to cut Army Group Don's remaining communications lines. To the south the Donetsk railroad was cut and on the 19th the Soviets reached the Sinelnikovo railroad junction 20 miles east-south-east of Dnepropetrovsk. By this time Army Group A had begun evacuating from the Taman Peninsula to reinforce Army Group South (as Hitler had renamed Army Group Don on 12 February), and von Manstein had initiated a series of manoeuvres that were to produce the last great German victory of the war.

He ordered the headquarters of the Fourth Panzer Army to move to Dnepropetrovsk to close the gap in the centre of the German line between the First Panzer Army and the southern flank of the former Army Group B (which had been divided between Army Group Centre and South). He then set about preparations for a counter-attack against the Russian salient that had formed at Kharkov. Despite the inherent risks of advancing in the spring thaw, both Hausser and von Manstein knew that the Soviet offensive was losing momentum, and that their lines of supply were now dangerously outstretched and the troops were tired from months of relentless fighting. Von Manstein asked for and received 12 tank divisions — the largest concentration of armour the Germans had thus far fielded — for an armoured counter-attack. He envisaged an assault from three sides, with the SS-Panzer Corps at the head of a pincer movement that would destroy the Russian divisions around Kharkov. While still ostensibly a Panzergrenadier division, *Leibstandarte* had already been strengthened by SS-Panzer Regiment 1, and with it a Tiger company — designated 13th (Heavy) Company of SS-Panzer Regiment 1.

The assault began on 23 February in a south-easterly direction, and on 28 February, after five days of bitter fighting, the spearhead units made contact with Fourth Panzer Army. *Leibstandarte*, and the entire body of the SS-Panzer Corps, then swung into action towards Kharkov itself. The Fourth Panzer Army reached Kharkov itself on 11 March, trapping several Soviet divisions, and after days of bitter fighting through the city, Kharkov was retaken on 14 March. The battle cost the Soviets 20,000 dead or wounded, together with 600 tanks. Casualties were also high on German side. The SS-Panzer Corps lost 12,000 killed or wounded and *Leibstandarte* alone suffered the loss of 167 officers and 4,373 NCOs and soldiers — 44 percent of its fighting strength. The army took its advance 30 miles farther north and on

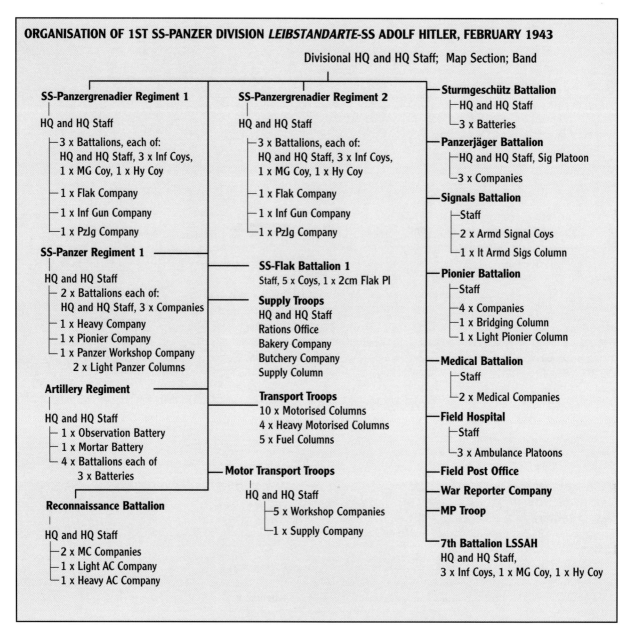

ORGANISATION OF 1ST SS-PANZER DIVISION *LEIBSTANDARTE*-SS ADOLF HITLER, FEBRUARY 1943

Divisional HQ and HQ Staff; Map Section; Band

SS-Panzergrenadier Regiment 1

HQ and HQ Staff
- 3 x Battalions, each of:
  HQ and HQ Staff, 3 x Inf Coys,
  1 x MG Coy, 1 x Hy Coy
- 1 x Flak Company
- 1 x Inf Gun Company
- 1 x PzJg Company

SS-Panzer Regiment 1

HQ and HQ Staff
- 2 x Battalions each of:
  HQ and HQ Staff, 3 x Companies
- 1 x Heavy Company
- 1 x Pionier Company
- 1 x Panzer Workshop Company
  2 x Light Panzer Columns

Artillery Regiment

HQ and HQ Staff
- 1 x Observation Battery
- 1 x Mortar Battery
- 4 x Battalions each of
  3 x Batteries

Reconnaissance Battalion

HQ and HQ Staff
- 2 x MC Companies
- 1 x Light AC Company
- 1 x Heavy AC Company

SS-Panzergrenadier Regiment 2

HQ and HQ Staff
- 3 x Battalions, each of:
  HQ and HQ Staff, 3 x Inf Coys,
  1 x MG Coy, 1 x Hy Coy
- 1 x Flak Company
- 1 x Inf Gun Company
- 1 x PzJg Company

SS-Flak Battalion 1
Staff, 5 x Coys, 1 x 2cm Flak Pl

Supply Troops
HQ and HQ Staff
Rations Office
Bakery Company
Butchery Company
Supply Column

Transport Troops
10 x Motorised Columns
4 x Heavy Motorised Columns
5 x Fuel Columns

Motor Transport Troops

HQ and HQ Staff
- 5 x Workshop Companies
- 1 x Supply Company

Sturmgeschütz Battalion
- HQ and HQ Staff
- 3 x Batteries

Panzerjäger Battalion
- HQ and HQ Staff, Sig Platoon
- 3 x Companies

Signals Battalion
- Staff
- 2 x Armd Signal Coys
- 1 x lt Armd Sigs Column

Pionier Battalion
- Staff
- 4 x Companies
- 1 x Bridging Column
- 1 x Light Pionier Column

Medical Battalion
- Staff
- 2 x Medical Companies

Field Hospital
- Staff
- 3 x Ambulance Platoons

Field Post Office

War Reporter Company

MP Troop

7th Battalion LSSAH
HQ and HQ Staff,
3 x Inf Coys, 1 x MG Coy, 1 x Hy Coy

18 March, the SS-Panzer Corps retook Byelgorod, thus regaining the defensive line of the Donets to Byelgorod, and correcting the tactical situation brought about by the Stalingrad disaster.

Previously, on 9 March, SS-Werfer Abteilung 102/502 (a Nebelwerfer unit) was assigned to the division, and shortly after taking Kharkov SS-Brigade Schuldt was disbanded. Despite the enormous losses, Kharkov was a timely victory, gained in no small part through the efforts of *Leibstandarte*. In every other theatre on every front the German armies were in retreat, and its propaganda value was immense. The red square in Kharkov was even renamed '*Leibstandarteplatz*' in the division's honour and on 21 March, Hitler awarded Dietrich Swords to his Knight's Cross.

It should be noted that, postwar, Soviet authorities alleged that *Leibstandarte* troops massacred 700 wounded Soviet troops in their hospital beds.

The late spring on the Eastern Front was quiet, a respite that afforded the division desperately needed time for rest and refitting. While attached to the reserve of Army Detachment Kempf in the Kharkov area, 2,500 Luftwaffe troops were transferred-in allowing time in May for some of the Leibstandarte veterans to visit their homes in Germany.

KURSK—OPERATION 'ZITADELLE'

Since June 1941, German attention had centred on the Russian front, but in the early months of 1943 the strategic situation began to change. The defeat of Rommel's Africa Korps in North Africa brought with it the prospect of an

Above: An SS motorcycle crew relaxes. The extreme cold, tiredness and the effort needed to ride the machine with its sidecar under these conditions is evident in the exhausted appearance of the rider and his passenger, April 1943.

invasion of Italy, and with the launching of daylight raids on the Ruhr by the USAAF 8th Air Force, German industrial production was threatened. There was also the looming threat of a Second Front in north-west Europe. So, although the Kharkov victory did much to restore German morale, with attention and resources now focused elsewhere no German commander believed that the next summer would see significant gains in Russia. However, on a limited level, the failure of Hitler's defensive doctrine during the winter had produced a substantial bonus, in that the long winter retreats had dramatically shortened the front and created a surplus strength on the Eastern Front equivalent to two armies. These two factors offered von Manstein and the OKH the temptation of an attack on the Soviet salient centred on Kursk. Although there was enthusiasm for the prospects of an incisive victory, most favoured defence. There were sharp divisions at the top, and even Hitler prevaricated. Some argued for the construction of an East Wall, a permanent line of fortifications across the USSR, and small local attacks that would wear down the Red Army. Guderian, recalled to active duty, told Hitler at a meeting on 9 March: 'The task for 1943 is to provide a certain number of tank divisions with complete battle efficiency capable of making limited objective attacks.'

Guderian's opinion, that only in 1944 would the Germans be able to go on the offensive again as the present situation showed that the divisions were much too weak, was shared by almost the entire senior army command. Von Manstein thought differently, believing it essential to deal the Soviet Army a series of powerful blows, and remove the Soviet threat to the Ukraine and Crimea. For three months Hitler deliberated, before finally deciding that he needed one more big victory in Russia, 'that will shine like a beacon around the world.' On 12 June he finally announced that he intended to execute Operation '*Zitadelle*' (Citadel).

The plan for 'Zitadelle', developed by Hitler with Kurt Zeitzler, the OKH Chief of Staff, in March, projected converging strikes by Ninth Army (Walther Model, Army Group Centre) and Fourth Panzer Army (Hoth, Army Group South) on the northern and southern flanks of the Kursk salient to achieve a double envelopment. Hitler favoured a large build up of men and material for a great attack in the future, which Guderian bitterly contested. He insisted upon the need for immediate action, arguing that further delay would allow the Russians time to build further strength. Zeitzler shared von Manstein's beliefs, and these were presented to Hitler on a number of times after 19 March. When the attack was postponed by Hitler, Zeitzler and von

Above: The PzKpfw IIs and IIIs (seen here) were obsolescent by the time of Kursk but *Leibstandarte* still had some on strength in spring 1943.

Below: A StuG 40 heavy assault gun moves forward, August 1943. The long-barrelled 75mm StuK 40 was an improvement on the StuG III's StuK 37 and started reaching units in 1942. Note the condition of the *Schürzen*.

Manstein became increasingly sceptical, and privately the Führer himself expressed his reservations.

They were well-founded. Prewarned of the German intentions by intelligence sources (the 'Lucy' spy ring), the Soviet forces under Georgi Zhukov were able to fortify the salient heavily, preparing defences in depth as well as building up massive troop concentrations in the area. Those defences consisted of six defensive belts, complete with some 22,000 guns, 3,306 tanks, vast minefields and trenches, manned on the northern half of the salient by Konstantin Rokossovsky's seven armies and in the southern half by Nikolai Vatutin's six armies, which included a tank army and two Guards tank armies. The Germans planned to assault the salient with 43 divisions, of which 17 were armoured, and two tank brigades, grouped in the Ninth and Fourth Panzer Armies.

The defenders were of a much stronger calibre than in 1941, and well equipped. The Germans however, were not only losing manpower, but also firepower. While a 1941 Panzer regiment had three battalions of about 70 tanks, a 1943 Panzer regiment had only two battalions of about 50 tanks, with a third battalion equipped with some 30 Sturmgeschütz IIIG vehicles. The tanks themselves were admittedly of much better quality. The mainstays, the PzKpfw II and III, were now being slowly replaced by numbers of the PzKpfw IV series and, more importantly, by PzKpfw V Panther and PzKpfw VI Tiger tanks, but these were untried in battle and the latter had had a disastrous debut. The heavy company of the *Leibstandarte* had 12 Tigers ready for the assault, with 72 PzKpfw IVs, 16 PzKpfw IIIs and IIs and 31 assault guns. The SS-Panzer Corps had a total of 425 tanks with 110 assault guns.

In June Dietrich finally handed over command of *Leibstandarte* to Teddy Wisch. Promoted to the unique rank of SS-Obergruppenführer und Panzergeneral der Waffen-SS, upon returning to Berlin he set about creating I SS-Panzer Corps from elements of *Leibstandarte* and 12th SS-Panzergrenadier Division *Hitler Jugend*. It was perhaps inevitable that so able a commander, and an unshakeable supporter of the Führer, would rise through the hierarchy, even if by this time he had begun publicly to express his doubts about the likelihood of a decisive victory in the east.

For the attack on the Kursk salient, already badly compromised, *Leibstandarte* was again part of Hausser's II SS-Panzer Corps, Fourth Panzer Army, which was to drive through the Soviet defences on the Voronezh front before turning north-east to take Prokharovka, where a decisive action was expected. II SS-Panzer Corps was assigned the left flank of the Fourth Panzer Army attack, and *Leibstandarte* was to assault in its centre. On its left was the elite Wehrmacht Panzer division *Grossdeutschland*, part of XXXXVIII Panzer Corps. Having been brought up to full strength, at the end of June the division began the march to the SS-Corps troop staging area north of Tomarovka.

The attack was launched at 03:30hrs on 5 July. On the southern spearhead the three SS divisions moved on three parallel lines of advance. Fighting through the heavy minefields north of Byelgorod, *Leibstandarte* was by 19:30hrs on the southern outskirts of Jakovleva, a village within the second defensive line some 14 miles into Soviet territory, and had already suffered 97 killed and 522 wounded. In the north, Model's Ninth Army ran into difficulties in the thickly sown minefields that were heightened by the loss of over three-quarters of his new Panthers through mechanical problems.

After a night marked by continuous infantry battles in pouring rain, at dawn the next day the SS divisions assaulted bunkers and fortified positions in the second line of defensive works. In a day of heavy fighting, *Leibstandarte* armour engaged the 1st Guards Armoured Brigade, destroying a large part of it, and carrying the front line to Pokrovka, south-west of Prokharovka.

The following afternoon, having torn a large hole in the Soviet line, the push began to Oboyan, 37 miles south of Kursk on the River Psel. Second SS-Panzer Army moved north-east on the Teterevino–Prokharovka road, aiming at Prokharovka on the Kursk–Byelgorod railway, where the Soviets had already begun to concentrate their armour reserves. However, during the characteristically rapid advance, which had carried II SS-Panzer Corps some 25 miles deep into Soviet lines, the three Waffen-SS divisions became separated, and both corps flanks were left wide open as Kempf's armoured detachment, advancing on the right flank, and XXXXVIII Panzer Corps, on the left, fell behind. *Totenkopf* (Hermann Priess) was moved to the flanks, and the advance proceeded.

On 8 July the Soviet Fifth Guards Tank Army mounted an armoured counter-attack that aimed at cutting II SS-Panzer Corps' supply route on the Byelgorod–Oboyan road, but was savaged by the Luftwaffe. By the end of the day the Corps HQ was able to report that 290 Russian tanks had been destroyed in the three days of fighting, but the next day, the advance of the Ninth Army ground to a halt. II SS-Panzer Corps regrouped; *Das Reich* was placed on the defensive, and *Leibstandarte* was ordered to push onwards.

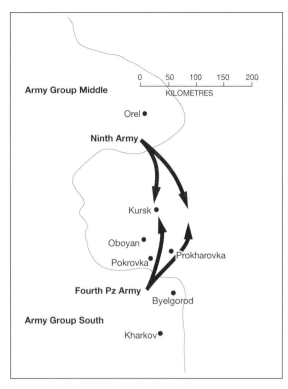

Above: The Battle of Kursk, 29 June–29 July 1943. The biggest tank battle of the war to date, by the end of it the SS-Panzer Corps would have its disposal only 30 PzKpfw VI Tigers, 69 PzKpfw IVs, 80 PzKpfw IIIs, four PzKpfw IIs and 64 assault guns along with a number of command vehicles and captured T-34s.

Below: Supported by a Tiger, infantry of the Waffen-SS move across uneven ground advancing against the enemy.

Above: The epitome of an *Ostkampfer*—an East Front fighter—August 1943.

Below: Wearing loose white covers to help him blend into the snow-covered terrain, this Waffen-SS Unterscharführer poses for the camera somewhere on the Eastern Front.

On the 10th, *Totenkopf* moved from the left to rejoin the *Leibstandarte* and *Das Reich* in the van for the assault on Prokharovka. Fighting through a sea of mud to the banks of the Psel River, to the west of the town and the last natural obstacle before Kursk, SS formations had by late afternoon assaulted across the river and were in position to attack the rear of the Soviet concentration. To the south III Panzer Corps began battling toward Prokharovka, attempting to link up with II SS-Panzer Corps before more Soviet reserves could be brought up.

On the plain outside the small town scene the forces massed for the largest tank battle yet seen, and the final decisive encounter on the Eastern Front. For the battle the Germans fielded some 600 tanks, and the Russians about 850, and with III Panzer Corps threatening from the south a pre-emptive strike was clearly advantageous to the Soviet commander, Vatutin. On 12 July Rotmistrov's Fifth Guards Tank Army launched a series of unco-ordinated strikes with the intention of separating the SS divisions. In an area of only a few square miles, firing at almost point-blank range across the dust-choked plain, the superior range of the German tank guns counted for nothing against suicidal attacks by Soviet tank crews. In the heavy fighting that ensued, the heavy company (the 13th) of *Leibstandarte*'s Panzer Regiment 1 engaged the Russian 181st Tank Regiment, and destroyed the whole unit without loss — but on both sides the losses were enormous. At the end of the day a thick pall of smoke hung over the wrecks nearly 700 tanks, nearly half of those engaged.

The Soviet attack was driven off, albeit with tremendous losses of men and materiel, and the Germans now held the area around Prokharovka and the railroad. III Panzer Korps managed to break through the Soviet line to the south that same day, but too late to effect the Kursk battle. Nevertheless, with the advance of the Fourth Panzer Army gathering pace, Von Manstein felt that he was close to success, so 13 July saw no let-up in the fighting at Kursk. While *Leibstandarte* rested, the *Totenkopf* and *Das Reich* divisions, attacked between Pravorot and Prokharovka, exploiting a gap in the enemy lines.

In the north, however, the Soviets had launched a strong counter-attack behind the Ninth Army north of Orel, which threatened to cut off the salient, forcing Model to redeploy forces and halting his advance. With the situation in the north around Orel becoming increasingly precarious, Hitler cancelled 'Zitadelle' on 13 July. There were still 80 miles, filled with defensive structures and Russian armour, between the two arms of the pincer, and the strength of the Soviet reserves could only be guessed at. Furthermore, on 10 July Allied troops had landed on Sicily, and the Soviets were threatening the Donets basin. To counter both of these threats Hitler needed troops. Although operations continued in von Manstein's sector, and II SS-Panzer Corps managed to link up with III Panzer Corps and destroy several Soviet units, heavy rainfall brought the advance, and German hopes of victory, to a halt on the night of 15 July.

At Kursk *Leibstandarte* paid heavily — 2,753 casualties, including 474 dead, and 19 tanks knocked out, or over 30 percent of its armoured strength. In total Hausser lost 420 of his tanks, while for the campaign Army Group South alone had expended 20,700 men killed and wounded. Soviet losses included 2,100 tanks, and the number of killed and wounded can only be guessed at. But having taken the initiative, the Soviets ensured there was no let up. In the immediate wake of the battles around Kursk, the Soviet commanders launched fierce counter-attacks against the Bryansk–Orel railway line that forced Model to withdraw from the Orel salient by 26 July.

In Italy a fresh emergency soon arose. In the wake of the Allied landings, the Fascist Grand Council led by Marshal Badoglio had begun secret negotiations with the Allies, and on 25 July it deposed Mussolini. Hitler was determined not to allow the Allies bases from which to attack the Romanian oilfields and expose his southern flank, and had already issued a contingency plan on 22 May, code-named Operation 'Alarich', that provided for the occupation of northern Italy and evacuation of the southern peninsula in the event of Italian capitulation to the Allies. In fact the negotiations between Italy and the Allies were protracted, allowing Hitler time to complete his occupation of Italy in September. On 3 August, as part of Alarich and against the bitter opposition of the front commanders, *Leibstandarte* was sent to Italy. Before entraining, it was stripped of all its remaining tanks, which passed over to *Das Reich* and *Totenkopf*, which now comprised the III SS-Panzer Corps. *Leibstandarte* then moved into Italy from Austria via the Brenner Pass, and occupied Bolzano. August passed on occupation duty in Milan, where the division was assigned new armoured vehicles, and helped to disarm surrendering Italian troops in the Po Valley.

In early August a strong Russian attack was launched by General Rodion Malinovsky's forces at the sector from which the Fourth Panzer Army had launched the attack against the Kursk salient. Malinovsky's attack tore a 35-mile wide gap in the German line. Through this breach the Russians poured, taking Byelgorod on 5 August and heading south-west toward the Dnieper River. As the fighting retreat continued along the Central Front towards Bryansk, Smolensk and Roslavl, Hitler finally accepted that retreat on the Eastern Front was inevitable and ordered work to begin on the defensive line (the 'Eastern Wall') previously suggested to him. This which was to run from Melitopol in the south to the shores of the Gulf of Finland at Narva — and it was to prove as unsuccessful as the Western Wall.

In the last two weeks of August the Soviet offensive was expanded to the north and south, where Fedor Tolbukhin's Southern Front drove in across the Donets south of Izyum and on the Mius River east of Snigrevka to threaten an envelopment of Army Group South. To the north, Kharkov was abandoned on 22 August and in the following week Army Group Centre's front was penetrated in three places. At the end of the month, the German Sixth Army withdrew from the Mius to the Kalmius, and three days later Army Group A began evacuating from the Taman peninsula.

Through the autumn the Soviet drive continued west, and on 15 September, with the northern flank of Army Group South threatening to disintegrate and the Soviets pressing at Smolensk, Hitler gave permission for the two army groups to retreat to the line of the Dnieper, Sozh and Pronya rivers. In most places the retreat was already underway, and in the last week of the month, as Bryansk, Smolensk and Roslavl were retaken, it developed into a race for the river lines.

Below: The north of Italy — *Leibstandarte* was transferred here on 1 August 1943 following the invasion of Sicily. The operation to take and hold north Italy proved remarkably successful. *Leibstandarte* left for Russia again in November, but the forces that remained showed that the thought that Italy would prove the 'soft underbelly of Europe' for Mark Clark's Fifth Army was entirely incorrect. In spite of Allied air superiority the German defence of North Italy proved dogged and efficient and the Germans would still hold some Italian territory in 1945.

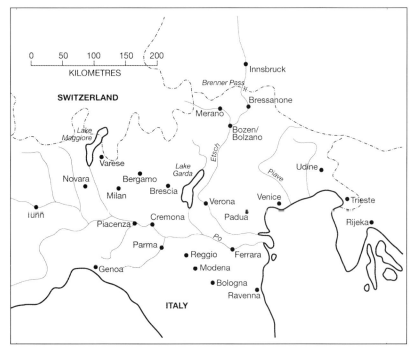

Above: Waffen-SS Grenadiers riding on the back of a Panzer IV. Apart from the dangers of the enemy and weather, troops travelling on the engine deck of tanks had another enemy — carbon monoxide poisoning, not unknown in Russia.

Above right: A welcome stop. A column of Waffen-SS motorcyclists pause during an exhausting move.

Below right: A stretcher bearer photographed during the Battle for Byelgorod.

Leibstandarte, stationed in northern Italy as part of II SS-Panzer Corps, was enjoying a welcome respite in the Italian sun. The sojourn was not without incident. Shortly after the surrender of the Italian government on 8 September, a detachment of the regiment was involved in Operation '*Eiche*' (Oak), the daring mountaintop rescue of Mussolini from captivity at the Campo Imperatore hotel on the Gran Sasso d'Italia high in the Abruzzi Apennine mountains.

On 19 September, reacting to a report that renegade Italian troops had captured two SS officers and were planning to attack the division, SS-Standartenführer Jochen Peiper shelled the town of Boves, killing 34 Italian civilians. Postwar, Italian authorities accused Peiper of war crimes for the attack, but the charges were dropped for lack of evidence. Further allegations were made that divisional troops helped round up Jews around Lake Maggiore for transfer to concentration camps: again these are as yet unconfirmed.

DEFENCE ON THE DNIEPER

The Dnieper River offers the strongest natural defensive line in western European Russia, but the losses incurred in battles to the east of the river denied Hitler the resources adequately to man and fortify the line and, coupled with the fact that the Red Army had established five bridgeheads over the river, the position the German armies held was at best tenuous. The stark reality of the situation was that in just two and a half months Army Group Centre and South had been forced back for an average of 150 miles on a front 650 miles long, and in so doing, had lost the most valuable territory taken during the advances of 1941–42. As for the East Wall, nothing had been done. Much of the proposed line had yet to be even surveyed.

After a brief interlude in the first week of October, as the Russians paused to regroup and bring up new forces, 45 divisions of the 4th Ukrainian Front attacked the Sixth Army positions between Melitopol and the Dnieper, and in three weeks it was driven back onto the lower Dnieper, trapping the Seventeenth Army in the Crimea. On 15 October a fresh onslaught began, this time at the First and Eighth Panzer Armies south of Kremenchung. Here the Soviets threw the full weight of the 2nd and 3rd Ukrainian Fronts, opening a 200-mile wide bridgehead between Cherkassy and Zaporozhe, while to the south the 3rd Ukrainian Front threatened important iron and manganese mining areas near Krivoi Rog and Nikopol. Then, south of the bridgehead at the confluence of the Pripyat and Dnieper, the Soviets broke out of two smaller bridgeheads and on 6 November, Kiev was retaken by the 1st Ukrainian Front, creating a large salient in the front.

In November *Leibstandarte* was ordered back to the Eastern Front. It travelled via Lvov to Ternopol as part of XXXXVIII Corps of the Fourth Panzer Army, and was rushed east into positions on the southern flank of the Kiev salient for a counter-attack that aimed at Zhitomir, and the Soviet bridgehead on the Dnieper. The attack was launched on 19 November and initially it achieved some success. Zhitomir was taken, and although it would soon have to be relinquished, Soviet supply routes between the city and Kiev were cut. Next *Leibstandarte* moved on Brusilov, where it met a strong concentration of V and VIII Guards Armoured Corps, and I Guard Cavalry Corps. With the 1st Panzer and 9th Panzer Divisions attacking the northern and southern flanks, and *Leibstandarte* from the west, on 24 November the concentration was encircled and destroyed. But despite inflicting substantial losses on the enemy, the Germans were unable, for lack of manpower, to hold the positions they captured and carry the advance further. On 16 December, amid biting cold and blinding snowstorms the division advanced east with the 1st and 7th Panzer Divisions from Korosten, aiming at encircling the Soviet armies around Meleni. This was achieved, but with so few troops that the positions could not be held and soon attack turned to retreat.

As the year drew to a close, the Fourth Panzer Army was pushed back west and south of the city by a fresh offensive launched on Christmas Eve by the combined forces of four Russian armies plus two independent corps of the 1st Ukrainian Front against the southern rim of Kiev. The next day it developed a second thrust west, which threatened to destroy the entire left flank of Army Group South, and succeeded in recapturing Zhitomir and the road linking it to Kiev. While recognising that this thrust could be employed to drive the two army groups back against the Black Sea and the Carpathian Mountains, Hitler saw that the southern attack posed the danger of an envelopment of Army Groups South and A between the Dnieper and Dniester Rivers, and considered it the greater danger. Fourth Panzer Army was ordered to bring it to a halt.

Although December had brought some respite, enabling the German forces to regain some of their balance, the best solution to the German predicament at this stage would have been to order Army Group South to withdraw to the next major line of defence, the Bug River. This Hitler would not consider, and instead the armies were told to hold their positions for the winter, and informed that they would have to do so without extra resources that were needed for defence against the expected invasion of north-west Europe. And so, now in the third winter of the Russian campaign, the men of *Leibstandarte* could again reflect on a year in which they had time and again been used to reinforce weak points in the German lines and incurred huge losses, many of them from the experienced core of veterans.

As the war in the east entered its fourth year, Zhukov's 1st Ukrainian Front moved across the Dnieper against Kirovgrad, taking advantage of the now severely weakened Army Group South right flank. Two days later Kirovgrad was in Russian hands, despite spirited defence by 11 German divisions. Fighting a continuing series of defensive engagements in the area around Zhitomir, Korosten and Beredichev, *Leibstandarte* at Beredichev temporarily checked the Soviet advance. By mid-January the Soviet First Tank Army, spearheading the 1st Ukrainian Front's southern advance, had gained 65 miles and was approaching Uman. In knee-deep mud, sleet and blizzards, Army Group South fought desperately to prevent its front from collapsing.

A new attack, begun on 25 January by Koniev's 2nd Ukrainian Front, in four days linked up with Vatunin's 1st Ukrainian Front and encircled six German divisions totalling 100,000 men at Korsun-Shevchenkovsky, north-west of Cherkassy. Hitler

Above: On the Eastern Front, March 1944. A messenger checks his horse's hooves prior to mounting. For all the attempts to motorise the army, Germany forces used more horses in World War II than World War I.

Below: Dutch SS Volunteers manning a 20mm flak gun in the ground role, July 1944. By the pile of expended ammunition at right they have seen heavy action. Dutchmen would make up two SS-Freiwilligen Divisions formed in 1945 — the Panzer Division Nederland and the Grenadier Division Landstorm Nederland

refused to countenance any breakout attempt, insisting that von Manstein instead link up with the trapped forces and thus re-establish the Dnieper line.

For the rescue attempt von Manstein concentrated most of his tank strength in XXXXVI and III Panzer Corps, and attached *Leibstandarte* to the latter. On 11 February the breakout began, with *Leibstandarte* attacking on the northern flank with the 1st, 17th and 16th Panzer Divisions assaulting to the south. Conditions could not have been worse with thick fog and heavily bogged roads rendering rapid movement virtually impossible. Zhukov threw in the Fifth Guards Tank Army to counter the German thrust and halted the northern flank when it was barely eight miles from the trapped pocket. Realising that the link-up he envisaged had failed, Hitler consented to a break-out attempt on 16 February, and that night a slow-moving column formed. Leaving the wounded and most of their equipment behind, 35,000 men began moving toward III Panzer Corps positions south-west of Dzhurzhentsky. Men of the *Leibstandarte*, covering the retreat, exhibited considerable bravery. In one documented incident two NCOs of the 6th Company, 2nd Panzergrenadier Regiment, held off two companies of Soviet troops before they could be relieved. In all 32,000 troops escaped from the pocket, about half of the number that had been trapped. Had it been totally surrounded Army Group South would almost certainly have been destroyed.

At the end of the month Army Groups South and A held a weak but almost continuous line about halfway between the Dnieper and the Bug. Its actions at Cherkassy and in holding this line left *Leibstandarte* badly mauled. Pulled back into the line north-east of Uman to face the advance of the 1st Ukrainian Front, by 28 February, it had only three tanks and four assault guns operational.

These straits afflicted all of von Manstein's divisions. In a pitifully weakened state they faced a mighty assault by the 1st, 2nd, and 3rd Ukrainian Fronts between the Pripet Marshes and the Carpathian mountains early in March, and in the north were driven behind the 1939 Polish border nearly to Kovel. In the centre the attack fell on Eighth Army east of Uman and in the south drove through the centre of the Sixth Army below Krivoi Rog. Manstein was obliged to make a gradual withdrawal to the Dniester River on the border with Romania, but Hitler's insistence on holding the mines near Nikopol and Krivoi Rog meant that by the end of the month the Sixth Army had nearly been encircled. On the left flank, the Soviet advance in the vicinity of Shepetovka opened a gaping hole in the German line. *Leibstandarte*, fighting as part of XXIV Corps, was unable to stem the onslaught, and by 15 March, the division had been all but annihilated — less than 1,250 men remained. In the last week of the month, together with the whole of the First Panzer Army, it was encircled at Kamenets-Podolski. Precious fuel and supplies were airlifted in to the pocket, and on 27 March, as the 4th Panzer Division (with 9th SS-Panzer Division *Hohenstaufen* and 10th SS-Panzer Division *Frundsberg*) launched a diversionary attack, the remnants of *Leibstandarte* fought out of the pocket to the west. By mid-April it was safely back in German lines.

THE WESTERN FRONT

On 18 April the division, although what remained scarcely warranted the name, entrained for north-western France for rest and refitting, to counter the expected summer invasion of north-west Europe. From 25 April it was headquartered at Turnhout, Belgium, as one of the elements of Dietrich's newly created I SS-Panzer Corps which was given the title *Leibstandarte* Adolf Hitler, with units at Hasselt and Herentals. Here over 2,000 troops were transferred into the division from the 12th SS Division, and on 3 May Hitler decreed new equipment for the division, much of it to come straight from the factory. With these and other replacements, by June 1944 *Leibstandarte* had been rebuilt to a strength of 20,000. However, it is worth noting that it was still some 208 officers and 2,234 NCOs and men below its notional establishment, and that the reinforcements were mostly raw recruits. In material strength, the division had 42–45 self-propelled guns, 48–50 PzKpfw IVs, 38 PzKpfw V Panthers, and 29 PzKpfw VI Tigers.

In early June, with German forces all along the Western Wall poised for the Allied invasion, which was expected to fall on the Pas de Calais, *Leibstandarte* was at Enghen, Belgium, on the reserve strength of OKH. For the invasion the Allies, under the command of General Eisenhower, had two army groups under Montgomery, plus an invasion fleet of 5,000 ships and most importantly a huge air armada that included 13,000 American aircraft alone. For the most part, with the exception of those who had fought in the desert and in Italy, the Allied soldiers were without experience, poorly trained and less politically motivated than their adversaries, particularly the SS infantrymen. The Allied soldier was also dependent on equipment untested in battle, tactics that were hopelessly outdated and had achieved nothing like the German level of co-ordination with armoured forces that were equipped with tanks greatly inferior to the Germans. It is hard to remember that the success of 'Overlord' was by no means a foregone conclusion. Crucial to the success were the elaborate deception operations (such as Operation 'Bodyguard') that preceded it, under which a fictitious army, the American First Army, was assembled in south-east England to reinforce the view held by von Rundstedt, C-in-C West, that the invasion would come in the Pas de Calais region. Thus on 6 June, when the Allies launched the second front in Normandy, Hitler still firmly believed that Normandy was merely a decoy operation to hide a larger invasion to come, and denied Rundstedt reinforcements for a counter-attack, instead relying on the two Panzer divisions in the area to face the weight of the combined air, sea and land offensive.

Severe moving sanctions were imposed on *Leibstandarte* and the 19 other divisions of the Fifteenth Army held in the Pas de Calais. *Leibstandarte*, as part of the strategic reserve, could not be called into action without the express permission of the Führer himself. The situation was further complicated by a muddled chain of command and communications, which meant that *Leibstandarte* was separated from the other elements of Dietrich's I SS-Panzer Corps — namely 12th SS-Panzer Division *Hitler Jugend*, 21st Panzer Division and Panzer Lehr. These had been transferred to the Normandy area prior to the invasion and, as the only three German divisions in the area, bore the full brunt of the initial assault. While *Leibstandarte* hurried to make ready its combat and supply vehicles for the move south, the *Hitler Jugend* became heavily involved in the fighting for Caen, 10 miles south-west of the mouth of the River Orne. The town and its surrounding heights were the primary target of the Anglo-Canadian forces at the eastern end of the invasion front over the first two weeks, but all attempts to capture the town were repulsed by stern defence, and the Allies suffered costly losses before they were be able to break out towards open terrain.

Above: A short pause in the fighting somewhere on the Eastern Front. Farm buildings burn in the background, behind this MG34 gunner. The experience gained by such troops on the Eastern Front meant that the fresh US and British troops coming ashore in Normandy faced forces with a proportion of veterans in their ranks. However, such was the attrition in Russia that the core of veterans was often quite small and the divisions were bulked out by well-motivated — and at this stage in the war still well-trained — but inexperienced troops.

ORGANISATION OF 1st SS-PANZER DIVISION *LEIBSTANDARTE*-SS ADOLF HITLER IN JUNE 1944

Divisional Staff; Map section; Band

SS-Panzergrenadier Regiment 1
- Regt HQ—HQ Company
  - 3 x Battalions
    - Battalion HQ
      - 5 x Infantry Companies
  - 16th Company (Flak)
  - 17th Company (Inf Gun)
  - 18th Company (Panzerjäger)
  - 19th Company (Recce)
  - 20th Company (Pionier)

SS-Panzer Regiment 1
- RHQ
- 2 x Battalions ea 5 x Companies
- 1 x Hy Company
- 1 x Pionier Company

SS-Panzer Artillery Regiment
- RHQ and HQ Company
- 4 x Abteilungen ea x 3 Batteries

SS-Panzer Recce Battalion 1
- HQ and HQ Company
  - 6 x Companies

SS Panzergrenadier Regiment 2
- Regt HQ—HQ Company
  - 3 x Battalions
    - Battalion HQ
      - 5 x Infantry Companies
  - 16th Company (Flak)
  - 17th Company (Inf Gun)
  - 18th Company (Panzerjäger)
  - 19th Company (Recce)
  - 20th Company (Pionier)

SS-Flak Battalion 1
Staff, 5 x Coys, 1 x 2cm Flak Platoon

Services Battalion
- Rations Office
- Bakery Company
- Butchery Company
- Rations Column

Supply Services
- Staff Division Service Officer
- 10 x Motor Vehicle Columns
- 4 x Large Motor Vehicle Columns
- 5 x Motor Vehicle Columns for fuel

Services Battalion
- STAFF
  - 5 x Workshop Companies
  - 1 x Supply Company

SS-Sturmgeschütz Battalion
- Staff
- 3 x Companies

SS Panzerjäger Battalion
- Staff
- 3 x Companies

SS-Panzer Signals Battalion
- Staff
- 2 x Panzer Telephone Company
- 1 x Lt Pz Signals Column

SS-Panzer Pionier Battalion
- Staff
- 4 x Companies

Medical Battalion
- Staff
- 2 x (mot) Med Companies

Field Hospital
- Staff
- 3 x Ambulance Platoon

Field Post Office

War Reporting Company

MP Troop

Note: On 24 September 1943, all Panzer divisions of the Heer (with the exception of 21st Panzer Division and Panzer Division Norwagen) were reorganised as Type 43 Panzer Divisions. Subsequently, the Waffen-SS expanded to 17 divisions, seven corps, plus miscellaneous guard, support and special forces troops, and on 22 October, the division was renamed 1st SS-Panzer Division *Leibstandarte*-SS Adolf Hitler. A Sturmgeschütz battalion and a medical company were transferred to 12th SS Panzer Division *Hitler Jugend*

On 9 June, acting on intelligence based on a intercept of Allied radio traffic suggesting an imminent attack in the Pas de Calais, *Leibstandarte* was ordered to an assembly area of east of Bruges to meet the assault. But this too was, in fact, part of the deception plans. Finally, six days after the invasion Hitler ordered *Leibstandarte* to make all haste in its preparations and join *Hitler Jugend* near Caen, under the command of I SS-Panzer Corps.

Despite some significant successes, including the heavy defeat of the 7th Armoured Division at Villers-Bocage on the 13th at the hands of former *Leibstandarte* officer Michael Wittmann, now commander of the 2nd Company of the 101st Heavy Panzer Battalion of I SS-Panzer Corps, by the 21st the Allies had a secure bridgehead on the Normandy beaches, and vast quantities of men and materiel were flooding ashore. With the understrength German divisions in Normandy committed at Caen, the Americans were able to break out of their bridgehead on the 18th and take Cherbourg on 27 June. German troop and materiel movement across northern France was seriously hampered by the effective disruption of the transport network by Allied bombing, and *Leibstandarte*'s PzKpfw V Panther tanks could not be transported across France, to be unloaded at Rouen, until the last week of the month. Divisional HQ was established 15 miles south of Caen. Finally on 28 June the 1st Panzergrenadier Regiment arrived Caen, and on the next day *Leibstandarte* units reached the invasion front. But it was be another week before the division was up to full strength, robbing Dietrich of the opportunity to use *Leibstandarte* for a combined counter-attack with *Hitler Jugend* to push the Allies back onto the beaches. In the interim, *Hitler Jugend* suffered grievously in the face of a concerted attempt to take high ground to the west of Caen by the infantry and armour of British VIII Corps (Operation 'Epsom'), launched on 25 June and preceded by a massive bombardment from sea and air. Gradually the division was driven back and relinquished part of the city to the British, albeit at a heavy cost to the attackers.

On 6 July the Allies launched Operation 'Charnwood' to secure the rest of the city. *Leibstandarte*, along with other German units, was rushed to the British sector and until 9th was fully engaged in repulsing the attack, which cost the life of former *Leibstandarte* regimental commander and current *Hitler Jugend* commander Fritz Witt, killed in his HQ by naval gunfire.

Although he had been held again at Caen, this concentration of German forces in the Caen sector was much as Montgomery planned (according to his own account), as it allowed American preparations for a major breakout in the western sector to go unmolested. In their sector, the only Waffen-SS divisions available were 2nd SS-Panzer Division *Das Reich* and 17th SS-Panzergrenadier Division *Götz von Berlichingen*, which were without any of their heavy armour.

On 11 July, *Leibstandarte* took over the Caen sector from the seriously depleted *Hitler Jugend*. Here, over the coming week, it played its most crucial role in the Normandy battles. Beginning on 18 July, three British armoured divisions attempted to break through the gap between Caen and the eastern heights, across a small bridgehead over the Orne River and through the four lines of man-made and natural defences, then across the hills at Bourguebus and to the open ground beyond. The operation was preceded by a three-hour bombardment by some 2,500 Allied aircraft, followed immediately by the armoured assault. 'Goodwood' began well for the British, who seized all their primary objectives, but then *Leibstandarte* was rushed in from Falaise, south of Caen. Arriving late in the afternoon, *Leibstandarte* launched a counter-attack along with the 21st Panzer Division and the British attack was halted on the left flank. The next morning fighting was sporadic, and it appeared that 'Goodwood' had petered out, but in the early afternoon, having brought up reinforcements, the British attacked again. The armoured spearhead quickly overran the forward German units and pressed on, but as the leading tanks approached the hill at Bourguebus at 16:00hrs, they came under accurate and concerted fire by the Panthers and PzKpfw IVHs of *Leibstandarte*, which had taken up positions on the hill itself. Heavy casualties were inflicted on the British 7th and 11th Armoured Divisions.

Inevitably, the weakened German defences began to lose the battle of attrition. Few reinforcements arrived, and free-roaming Allied aircraft destroyed supplies from the air before they could reach the lines and made movement by day in the maze of narrow lanes impossible. By the 21st, despite failing to break out of the Orne bridgehead, the Allies had expanded the bridgehead by some five miles and finally taken Caen from its defenders. *Leibstandarte* held firm defensive positions on the Caen–Falaise highway until the end of the month, against repeated Allied attacks. On the 28th, the number of killed, wounded, missing or captive

Above: On 31 July 1944 the Allies broke through the German lines around Avranches. Although badly mauled the battered SS divisions still proved to be dangerous opponents. This Wespe 105mm mounted on a PzKpfw II chassis was produced from 1943 and first saw action at Kursk.

Below: An SdKfz 231 eight-wheeled armoured car from the *Hitler Jugend* Division amidst the ruins of a French town. The 12th SS-Panzer Division *Hitler Jugend* was an attached unit to I SS-Panzer Corps during the Battle of Normandy.

**SUBSIDIARY UNITS OF
1st SS-PANZER CORPS
LEIBSTANDARTE ADOLF HITLER
IN NORMANDY, 1944**

Corps HQ I SS-Panzer Corps/101
Aircraft Staffel (Flight)
SS-Corps Map Unit
SS-Rocket Launcher Battery (mot)
    101/501
SS-Corps Signals Battalion 101/501
SS-Hy Observation Battery 101/501
SS-Military Geology Battalion 101
SS-Corps Supply Troops 101
SS-Lorry Company 101
SS-Corps Hospital Abteilung101
SS-Artillery Command I
SS-Artillery Battalion 101/501
SS-Flak Battalion 101
SS-Flak Company
SS-Ambulance Platoon 501
SS-Field Post Office (mot) 101
SS-War Reporting Company (mot)
SS-MP Company 101 (mot)
SS-Korps-Sicherungs-Kompanie 101
SS-Field Replacement Brigade
SS-Field Hospital 501

Attached units
1st SS-Panzer Division
    Leibstandarte-SS Adolf Hitler
12th SS-Panzer Division Hitler
    Jugend
Panzer Lehr Division (for the
    Normandy Campaign, 1944)
Heavy SS-Panzer Abteilung 101
    (501) (for the Normandy
    Campaign, 1944)

was 1,500 and Panzer strength stood at 33 PzKpfw V Panthers, 30 PzKpfw IVs and 22 Sturmgeschütz IIIs.

In the last week of July, the US forces launched Operation 'Cobra' from the vicinity of St Lô, a concerted attempt to break-out of the 'bocage' terrain that had stymied their advance, carrying Omar Bradley's First Army to Avranches at the base of the Cotentin Peninsula. At the beginning of August, Hitler ordered a German counter-attack, aimed at splitting the First Army, now commanded by Courtney Hodges, and Patton's Third. New reinforcements brought *Leibstandarte* strength up to 20,395. The plan called for two co-ordinated thrusts, one of which headed west towards Avranches, and the other in an encircling movement towards St Lô. Launched on the 6th, initially gains of a few miles were made, but it was soon halted by a murderous barrage of rocket fire by Allied fighter-bombers. On 7 August, under a blanket of protective cloud, *Leibstandarte*, together with four other SS-Panzer divisions and three Wehrmacht Panzer divisions, renewed the attack. *Das Reich* managed to recapture Mortain, and a *Leibstandarte* armoured battle group under Jochen Peiper advanced as far as Bourlopin, but was again stopped by massive concentrations of Allied aircraft. Another attempt was mounted the next day, but it too failed. The Canadian First Army then launched a powerful thrust south-west to Falaise, and an encirclement of the German forces threatened. Three days after it began the Avranches attack petered out, and *Leibstandarte* was pulled back into defensive positions at St Barthelemy.

On 13 August, *Leibstandarte* arrived at Argentan on the Orne, south-east of Falaise. The following day, with the noose tightening around Seventh Army in the 'Falaise Pocket', Dietrich again requested permission to pull back, but was refused. Encircled by the Allied forces, and under a hail of aircraft and artillery fire, Hausser, commander of Fifth Army, was told by von Kluge (who had succeeded von Rundstedt as Commander-in-Chief West) to withdraw II SS-Panzer Corps (*Hohenstaufen* and *Frundsberg*), his motors and his administrative personnel, and between 21 and 24 August *Leibstandarte* crossed the Seine near Elbeuf and was withdrawn to positions behind the river. Although 35,000 escaped from Falaise, some 50,000 other German troops and much of the equipment were captured.

Having jumped the Seine and captured Paris on 25 August, the Allies began the pursuit of the disorganised German forces across northern France and into Belgium. Already, on the 15th, supplementary landings had been made in the south of France between Cannes and Toulon (Operation 'Dragoon') in support of the Normandy invasion rendering the German position in France increasingly precarious. Pulled back through Marle and Montcornet, by the end of the month *Leibstandarte* reputedly had no tanks or artillery pieces and had suffered an estimated 6,000 casualties. There was no let up in the fighting. On 3 September there were minor defensive skirmishes with British troops in Philippeville, Fleurus and in Mons, Belgium, where the division was again threatened with encirclement, this time by the US First Army. Another 25,000 German troops fell captive, but *Leibstandarte* slipped through the net at Jodoigne, Tirlemont, Hasselt and Diest, and into the Bree–Neerpelt–Lommel Mol area. On 4 September, with the US Army preparing to cross the Meuse, *Leibstandarte* received orders to withdraw to the area around Bitburg, Germany, and into the defences of the Western Wall.

Despite three months of successful advances the Allies had yet to capture any of the Channel ports, and their overstretched supply lines ran all the way back to the Normandy coast. Thus at the beginning of September there was a notable loss of momentum, which allowed the Germans time to reorganise. Through the month, poorly conceived operations against Antwerp and three important Dutch river positions at Arnhem (Operation 'Market Garden') were successfully beaten off, as Montgomery and Patton engaged in a race to the Rhine that further stretched the supply lines. Von Rundstedt, who had been reappointed as C-in-C West by Hitler in an attempt to bolster morale, now marshalled the 63 depleted divisions along the Western Wall running along the line of the German/Dutch frontier for the defence of the homeland. Although this not was considered practicable by the field commanders, the alternative, a retreat to the Rhine, was not even considered by Hitler.

THE ARDENNES — OPERATION 'HERBSTNEBEL'

In fact, with the Allies halted in the north by II SS-Panzer Corps and in the south by a determined defence from 11th Panzer Division and several Volksgrenadier divisions, and the knowledge that the Allied supply lines had been overstretched, Hitler was already confidently preparing a counter-offensive at the southern flank of the US Third Army — the offensive was called Operation '*Herbstnebel*' or 'Autumn Mist'.

His ambitious plan, essentially a repeat of the 1940 offensive, centred on a rapid drive to Antwerp to split the British and American forces and stabilise his western front. Both von Rundstedt and Model voiced their reservations, but they were ignored. Thus through the late autumn and into December 25 German divisions, 11 of them armoured, secretly made ready for the offensive. For the attack they were arranged into three armies, under Dietrich, Manteuffel and Brandenberger. Dietrich's Sixth Panzer Army, commanding I (Herman Priess) and II (Willi Bittrich) SS-Panzer Corps, was by far the most powerful, and as the first wave tasked with the main effort of breaking through the US XVIII Corps' (Matthew Ridgway) lines in the Ardennes, seizing the high ground of Elsenborn Ridge and control of the roads in the north, and then moving to capture the vital bridges across the Meuse between

Below: Reinforcements being rushed forward to the Normandy front. The heavy camouflage on this PzKpfw IV reflects the problems caused by Allied air supremacy.

ORGANISATION OF 1st SS-PANZER DIVISION *LEIBSTANDARTE*-SS ADOLF HITLER IN AUTUMN 1944

SS-Kampfgruppe Hansen
1 x SS-Panzergrenadier Regiment
1 x SS-Panzerjäger Abteilung
    (21 x Jagdpanzer IV, 11 x 75mm PaK)
1 x Artillery Abteilung (towed 105mm guns, 24 x Nebelwerfers)

SS-Kampfgruppe Sandig
1 x SS-Panzergrenadier Regiment
1 x Flak Abteilung
1 x Nebelwerfer Abteilung
1 x Pionier Abteilung

SS-Kampfgruppe Knittel
1 x SS-Recce Battalion
1 x Battery towed 105mm guns
1 x SS- Panzer Pionier Company

SS-Kampfgruppe Peiper
1 x SS-Panzer Regiment (72 x PzKpfw V Panthers and PzKpfw IVHs)
1 x Heavy SS-Panzer Abteilung
(No 501 with 45 x Königtiger)
1 x Flak Abteilung (No 84)
1 x SS-Panzergrenadier Battalion
1 x SS-Panzer Artillery Battalion
1 x Sturmgeschütz Company
2 x SS-Panzer Pionier Companies
1 x SS-Panzer Signals Company

Liège and Huy. A second wave with Kurt Student's Fifteenth Army was then to advance on Antwerp, trapping four Allied armies in the north. Manteuffel's Fifth Panzer Army on the south-western flank aimed at Brussels, and Brandenberger's Seventh Army was to hold the southern flank. The start date was set at 16 December.

During late October and early November *Leibstandarte*, as part of LXVI Corps, Seventh Army, refitted at Osnabrück. New equipment was found, although munitions and fuel were becoming increasingly scarce, and 3,500 replacements, many of them with only a minimum of training, were drafted in. Between 9 and 18 November, assigned to Sixth SS-Panzer Army, the division assisted in rescue efforts to save German civilians at Köln (Cologne), after the devastating Allied bombing on the city. By December 1944, division strength was at 22,000 (estimated), 84 tanks, and 20 self-propelled guns Finally on 14 December the heavy veil of secrecy that had masked preparations for the winter offensive in the Ardennes lifted. I SS-Panzer Corps was placed at the spearhead between Hollerath and Krewinkel, with *Hitler Jugend* on the right and *Leibstandarte* on the left. *Leibstandarte*, now in the command of Wilhelm Mohnke, was instructed to divide into four Kampfgruppen, under Hansen, Sandig, Knittel and Peiper.

The attack began at first light on 16 December with a concerted artillery barrage on the American lines, thinly held by six divisions of resting and newly arrived troops. At spearhead of the I SS–Panzer Corps, Kampfgruppe Peiper — the most powerful Kampfgruppe — began moving through the heavy snow with Kampfgruppe Sandig following closely behind. Passing through the heavily wooded and congested Losheim Gap into Belgium, where 12th Volksgrenadier Division had swept aside weak defence, progress was at first slow, but by early evening the vanguard of *Leibstandarte* was past Losheim and moving west through more open terrain toward Lanzerath. Here it met with 9th Fallschirmjäger Regiment and struck out towards Buchholz railway station on the Buchholz–Honsfeld road. By first light on the 17th *Leibstandarte* was in Honsfeld, which it took with comparative ease.

But hour by hour, Pieper's limited fuel reserves were rapidly diminishing. Disregarding specific orders to avoid the area, he turned north toward the American fuel depot at Büllingen, bypassed Heppenbach and captured the depot, and 50,000 gallons of precious fuel with comparative ease. Pressured by accurate artillery fire, his Kampfgruppe moved out in two columns on the Büllingen–St Vith road shortly before midday, then toward Ligneuville on the route to Stavelot, taking Schoppen, Ondenval and Thirimont. South east of Malmédy *Leibstandarte* ran into Battery B of the US 285th Artillery Observation Battalion, who were quickly captured and herded into a field adjacent to a crossroads near Baugnez. According to the reports of survivors, at least 86 of them were subsequently executed when a passing SS soldier began firing into the group. When details of the massacre became public a few days later, Dietrich's headquarters ordered an investigation, but that met with denial. The incident is, perhaps, the most notorious of the atrocities for which *Leibstandarte* soldiers stood trial.

At Ligneuville, Peiper was delayed by a few American tanks but soon took the town. Continuing on towards Trois Ponts and Beaumont, at Stavelot the lead units met with fierce defence and were forced to wait for daybreak to carry on the advance. By 10:00hrs, after a heavy German artillery barrage, the Stavelot bridge was firmly in German hands. Peiper immediately headed for the three crossings — two over the Salm and one over the Amblève — in the Trois Ponts area, from where he intended to move on Werbomont. On 18 December Peiper's lead elements reached Stavelot and Trois Ponts on the north side of the Amblève. Moments before his arrival, the 291st Engineers had blown three bridges — one over the Amblève at Trois Ponts and two on the Salm River, south of Trois Ponts.

Peiper was now forced to turn north to La Gleize, rather than follow his planned crossing of the Amblève for the most direct route to the objective. To complicate matters further, the river on his left and the high wooded hills on the right limited his route of advance to the vulnerable valley road. In the late afternoon the fog that had hampered air operations cleared, and the battle group came under attack by fighter-bombers. These succeeded only in delaying the column, but on the night of 18/19 December Kampfgruppe Peiper was in woodland surrounding Stoumont, and appeared poised to break out of the valley and into the open country to the north.

Opposite: Troops of the Waffen-SS resting in the bocage of Normandy.

Below: Kampfgruppe Peiper's progress during the Ardennes campaign 16 December 1944–20 January 1945. Initially good progress was halted by tenacious American defence, although Peiper did secure much-needed fuel at Büllingen. He also had the opportunity to attack northwards from there to encircle the American divisions on the Elsenborn ridge. While this would probably have had no impact on the course of the campaign, it would certainly have had an immediate tactical effect.

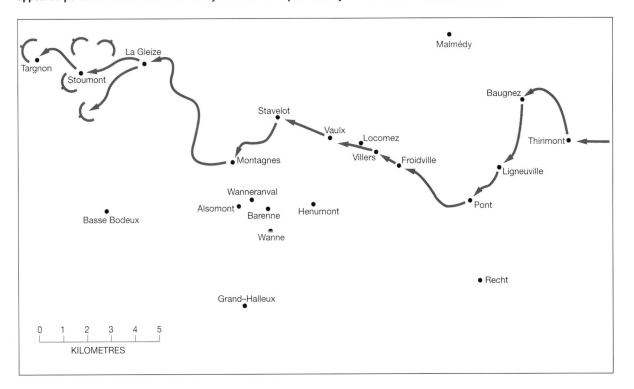

Above: Captured as he crouched in a foxhole this boy soldier was taken prisoner by a unit of the US Seventh Army. He claimed to be 14 years and seven months old and was one of the youngest soldiers captured by the American unit. He is wearing Waffen-SS garments with all the insignia removed.

It was, however, isolated at the head of a long salient and suffering another fuel crisis. Furthermore, Dietrich had still failed to capture the Elsenborn Ridge on the right flank and Allied HQ had woken up to full extent of the attack, which initially had been interpreted as a local attack on Monschau. As reinforcements were rushed into the line, opposition began to stiffen considerably.

Peiper moved on Stoumont on the morning of the 19th, where a desperate battle ensued with units of the 30th Infantry Division before the town was finally taken. Dangerously low fuel supplies now forced him to halt, unaware of the vast fuel depot located in the area. But as he waited at Stoumont for fuel and reinforcements to cross the Stoumont bridge and continue the drive, Stavelot was attacked by US troops, and by the evening the northern approach to the bridge had been destroyed. The noose was tightening on Peiper. Although he had found an intact bridge over the Amblève at Cheneux, his advance in that sector was halted by the 82nd Airborne Division, which had built a front on the south side of the Amblève extending east to the Salm.

Now trapped, Peiper sought and was refused permission to withdraw back to the *Leibstandarte* lines. A battalion of the 2nd SS-Panzergrenadier Regiment managed to reach him with vital fuel on foot via a footbridge across the Amblève east of Trois Ponts at Petit Spa, and on the afternoon of 22 December they attacked the US aid station at Petit Coo. Fierce fighting raged on into the night, but efforts to reinforce Peiper from the east and to retake Stavelot by other elements of the *Leibstandarte* on the 19th were beaten off and an attempt in mid-afternoon by the combined forces of Kampfgruppe Sandig's two battalions and Peiper's two Königstiger battalions, with a co-ordinated attack westward by Gustav Knittel's command, also failed under accurate and heavy artillery fire.

Abandoning its plans for attack, on 21 December Kampfgruppe Peiper withdrew to La Gleize, a small hamlet containing nothing more then a circle of white houses with a church and a schoolhouse, near to the vital Cheneux bridge. In the schoolhouse basement Peiper established his HQ, and was soon under fire from US heavy artillery located at Stoumont. In the streets savage battles finally forced the Germans back, and on 23 December Peiper was given permission to try to break out to the east, with the other elements of the *Leibstandarte* tasked with providing cover. Kampfgruppe Hansen reached Petit Spa and there tried to cross the Amblève river, but the bridge was blocked by a stricken tank and a push north was met by firmly entrenched American armour and infantry armed with anti-tank weapons.

Leaving behind 150 American prisoners and his wounded to destroy the remaining tanks, at 04:00hrs on Christmas Day Peiper and the 1,800-strong column was retreating along a small track that led into the Amblève valley to Le Venne (Wanne), south of Trois Ponts, and the *Leibstandarte* lines. Moving only in darkness, they paused for rest at daybreak, but were soon on the march again. There was more fighting with airborne troops from the 82nd Airborne Division, and a crossing of the cold, fast-flowing Salm River, before finally the 800 survivors of the Kampfgruppe, including an exhausted Peiper, stumbled into the German positions. Thus the exploits of the once mighty Kampfgruppe Peiper were ended, and with it the Sixth Army role in the Ardennes offensive. Starting with about 5,800 men, 60 tanks (some Tigers), three Flak tanks, 75 halftracks, 14 20mm Flak wagons, 27 75mm assault guns, plus 105 and 150mm SP howitzers, the group was now reduced to 800 survivors.

HUNGARY — OPERATION 'FRÜHLINGSERWACHEN'

Following the Soviet re-conquest of Romania in 1944, forces under Marshal Malinovsky advanced toward Hungary on two fronts, breaking through via Arad on 22 September and joining Petrov's 4th Ukrainian Front to launch a strong drive on the capital, Budapest. Outside Budapest Malinovsky stalled in bad weather, but on 3 December on the southern flank Tolbukhin's 3rd Ukrainian Front reached Lake Balaton, encircling the city. Still believing he could manipulate the situation in the east, in early January 1945 Hitler began to assemble a large concentration of SS divisions for an attack in the east, with the goal of stabilising the situation in Hungary and saving the link to the oil from wells near Lake Balaton. But on 12 January Soviet forces along the Vistula launched one of the greatest offensives of the war, aimed at driving the German army out of Poland. Heavily outnumbered, the Germans were forced to relinquish much of the country by the end of the month.

In Hungary the attack moved up the Danube Valley toward Budapest and Vienna, and drove most of the German forces out of eastern Hungary. In Budapest the SS garrison hung on tenaciously, and launched a series of failed counter-offensives. Three attempts to relieve it, including one by VI SS-Panzer Corps also failed. On 27 January the 3rd Ukrainian Front attacked and in mid-February the final German positions in the city were overrun.

With the 3rd Ukrainian Front now threatening the Balaton oilfields, in mid-February Sixth Panzer Army began transferring in from the Ardennes, and with it I SS-Panzer Corps. Rushed from the western front, *Leibstandarte* and *Hitler Jugend* were thrown into battle, with the objective of destroying the Seventh Guards Army bridgehead at Gran. Although between them they could muster only some 150 tanks

Below: Panzer IIIs and IVs and of the Waffen-SS passing a war photographer. Dietrich would say, towards the end, that his Sixth Panzer Army was so called because it had only six tanks left!

and assault guns, the bridgehead was smashed, and with it 8,500 Soviet troops. With Gran relieved and a threat on Vienna averted, the larger operation — aimed at destroying the Red Army between the Danube, the Plattensee and the Drava, and establishing a line east of the Balaton fields — could begin.

Immense secrecy surrounded the operation, codenamed 'Frühlingserwachen' (Spring Awakening). SS-Sturmbannführer Otto Günsche, Hitler's adjutant, briefed Dietrich verbally, and no reconnaissance was permitted. But the ambitious plan was already compromised by British intelligence. Tolbukhin, commander of 3rd Ukrainian Front, was briefed by Stavka that that the main thrust would come between the Plattensee and the Velenczsee, and in response ordered extensive defences to be laid. Here Dietrich's Sixth Panzer Army, renamed Sixth SS-Panzer Army after the Ardennes offensive and including I (Leibstandarte and Hitler Jugend) and II (Das Reich and Hohenstaufen) SS-Panzer Corps, two cavalry divisions and IV SS-Panzer Korps (Wiking and Totenkopf), was ordered to attack south, on either bank of the Sarviz Canal.

For the thrust Dietrich placed the Leibstandarte, now commanded by SS-Brigadeführer Otto Kumm, at the spearhead, with II SS-Panzer Corps to the left and I Cavalry Corps to the right. Kumm's goal was to cut the Russian communications across the Danube and, if successful, drive north for Budapest. For the attack he had 12,461 troops and 14 operational PzKpfw IVHs, 26 Pzkpfw V Panthers, and 15 Jagdpanzer IVs and StuG IIIGs. The heavy tank unit, SS-Panzerabteilung 501, had a mere four Königstigers battle ready.

Having moved into its positions, Leibstandarte began preliminary attacks on 3 March. The main assault was launched at dawn four days later. It was supposed to fall a day earlier, but to retain the element of surprise, troops were held 12 miles from their assembly areas and the long, tiring march through the mud created by an early thaw left them exhausted and in need of rest. Hitler's plan had not taken into account the appalling conditions created by an early thaw, in which normally frozen ground became heavily water-logged. Not even tracked vehicles could operate off the paved roads, and these inevitably became badly clogged with traffic. Dietrich reported after the war that 132 vehicles were trapped in the mud, and 15 Königstigers sank up to their turrets in the mire. Furthermore, there were shortages of ammunition.

Below: A member of the Waffen-SS lies dead in a field in France. Someone has searched through his pockets discarding what they considered of no interest or use.

Leibstandarte's I SS-Panzer Regiment made the deepest penetration and was only 20 miles from the Danube, its first objective, when the Russians counter-attacked on 16 March, trapping the overextended Sixth SS-Panzer Army. Das Reich fought and held open a narrowing pocket through which the trapped divisions escaped, but with Hungarians formations deserting en masse, the full weight of the Russian 2nd and 3rd Ukrainian Fronts was brought to bear on the SS formations. With the spectre of defeat hanging, a fighting retreat back to Germany and Austria began. But Hitler had decided to inflict another humiliation on the SS. Reacting to reports by Balck on 23 March that the men had lost confidence in their leaders who added that the Waffen-SS formations were on the brink of collapse, the

Führer in a fit of pique ordered the Waffen-SS divisions to remove their regimental honour titles.

Goebbels wrote in his diary: 'The Führer has decided to make an example of the SS formations. He has commissioned Himmler to fly to Hungary to remove their armbands . . . The indignation of the SS commanders in the field can well be imagined and Krämer, Dietrich's chief-of-staff, suggested asking Führer headquarters whether the armbands of the men killed between the Plattensee and the Danube should also be removed . . .' In the end, the order was never carried out. It did not go unnoticed, however, and Dietrich reportedly stated that he would sooner shoot himself than carry out such an order.

Little more than a week after they had launched the attack, the 2nd and 3rd Ukrainian Fronts broke through on either side of Lake Balaton and by the end of the month had crossed the border into Austria. General Lothar Rendulic, recently appointed the command of Army Group South, was told to hold Vienna and the Alpine passes. Dietrich's Sixth SS-Panzer Army, as part of the group, did what it could to defend the city with what little it had, but as the strength of the *Leibstandarte* and *Hitler Jugend* combined was down to only 1,600 men and 16 tanks Hitler's demands that the city be held to the last man were

Above: Guarded by Canadians, these youthful members of the Waffen-SS captured during the fighting in Normandy gave their ages as being between 16 and 20.

wishful thinking in the extreme. On 6 April the Red Army was on the outskirts of the city and by the middle of the month was approaching the centre, while to the north and south of the city the Soviets were threatening an envelopment.

Already, on 1 April, the Red Army had launched its last great offensive of the war, and sealed the fate of the Third Reich. With the Ruhr encircled and Silesia gone, tank, artillery and ammunition production at a mere ebb, and gasoline in hopelessly short supply, the only thing prolonging the war was the Führer, who grimly held on to hope for another miracle similar to the one that had saved Frederick the Great during the Seven Years' War. None was forthcoming, and on 16 April on the Oder–Niesse Line the 1st Belorussian and 1st Ukrainian Fronts broke through toward Berlin. On 21 April Sokolovski's 1st Belorussian Front reached Berlin and with the 1st Ukrainian moving from the south-east, by 24 April the city was encircled.

In mid-April *Leibstandarte* was forced back from Vienna by the advance of Malinovsky's 2nd Ukrainian Front, and retreated with the remnants of the Sixth Panzer Army to positions to the west of the city. In Berlin, loyal to the last, the honour guard battalion of the *Leibstandarte*, SS Guard Battalion I, commanded by Wilhelm Mohnke, battled hand-to-hand with the Soviet forces closing on Hitler's underground bunker. On 30 April Soviet troops entered the Reichstag and the Führer shot himself and his wife. Berlin surrendered two days later on the night of 6/7 May. Desperate to escape capture by vengeful Soviet troops, from whom they expected no quarter, what troops remained of Hitler's guard fled south toward US lines. Of the other elements of *Leibstandarte* Dietrich himself surrendered at Kufstein, south-east of Munich.

INSIGNIA, CLOTHING & EQUIPMENT

INSIGNIA

RZM — *Reichzeugmeisterei* — the Nazi HQ organisation based in Munich, oversaw the design and manufacture of all Nazi uniforms and insignia. Generally, SS insignia can be classified as follows (military speciality insignia, qualification badges, decorations and campaign medals are, for reason of brevity, excluded): national emblem, honour title cuffbands, shoulder straps, *Totenkopf* badge, SS runes, collar *Tresse*, rank insignia, camouflage insignia, vehicle insignia.

National emblem (*das Hoheitsabzeichen*)

The national emblem of the Third Reich was an eagle clutching a swastika in its talons, a version of which was worn by every uniformed organisation — military, political or civilian — in Germany. The SS in general wore the eagle mounted either on the top front of the officer's cap, above the capband, on the front or left side of soft crush caps, or more unusually on the upper left arm of the combat, service and walking-out dress.

Honour title cuff bands

Cuff bands bearing unit 'honour titles' were worn by at least 50 elite German army and Luftwaffe formations during the war. Names were chosen after geographical regions or racial designations, contemporary Nazi heroes or historical figures. The cuffband was a strip of black cloth about 3cm wide, and was worn on the left-hand sleeve of an SS greatcoat or tunic. The font used for the *Leibstandarte* cuffband was unique to the unit. Officers sometimes had their bands tailor-made — Dietrich had his 'Adolf Hitler' cuff embroidered in gold.

Shoulder boards

Shoulder straps were constructed of black wool material and secured to the shoulder by a loop at the shoulder seam and a button near the uniform collar. Officers wore the shoulder straps corresponding to their rank with appropriate pips and metal monograms. NCOs' shoulder straps were trimmed with *Tresse* and also displayed the appropriate pips. Depending on the unit, shoulder boards were trimmed with various colours — white for infantry, yellow for reconnaissance, pink for Panzer troops and so on. In addition, the *Leibstandarte* had a

Below: Shoulder boards showing the monogram 'AH' identifying the wearer as a member of the *Leibstandarte*.

Bottom: Different forms of *Leibstandarte* cuff title.

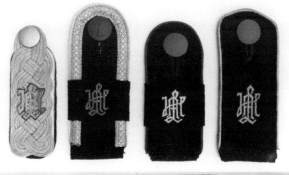

Above: Displayed is the enlisted and NCO grade peaked cap with leather chinstrap. The piping is white denoting infantry. The pavilion shows a very common 'front line crush' favoured by many NCOs. *Wade Krawczyk*

Right: Re-enactor showing off the uniform of a *Leibstandarte* (note cuff band) Panzergrenadier in front of a Russian T-34 tank. The man wears his *Zeltbahn* (the shelter quarter that doubled both as a poncho and as part of a pup tent) in a variation of 'Plane Tree' camouflage patterns. His weapon is an StG44 (StG=*Sturmgewehr*=assault rifle, the magazines for which are carried in canvas pouches (three each side) slung around his chest. Into his webbing are stuck two M24 stick grenades and an entrenching tool. In his left hand he holds a Tellermine 35 — usually detonated by a friction plate. His bayonet hangs from his belt and his gas mask container is slung over his shoulder with a grey cloth gas cape bag. *Peter Amodio*

special 'AH' (Adolf Hitler) shoulder board monogram, either of early (large) or late (small) style. NCO monograms were of silver metal, and officers' were gold metal.

SS Totenkopf (death's head)

The *Totenkopf* (death's head) symbol is, along with the SS double lightning bolts, the most distinctive of SS insignia. Its origins lay in the Prussian and Imperial German army, and during World War I it was used by the elite Brandenburger units. It was then appropriated by the Freikorps, and thereafter by the SS. Every SS unit wore the *Totenkopf* on the front of an officer's cap, in the centre of the headband or on the top front of soft crush caps. The *Totenkopf* was also the adopted symbol of the original concentration camp *Standarten* — which eventually became the 3rd SS-Panzer Division *Totenkopf*.

SS Runes

The 'Sig' rune is an ancient Germanic symbol of Thor, the Norse god of thunder, and is representative of a lightning bolt. It was designed in 1933 by Walter Heck, who used a double sig rune as a visual alliteration to the double 'ss' in Schutzstaffel. Waffen-SS troops of purely German heritage (*Reichsdeutsche*) were permitted to wear the SS runes on the right collar patch. Waffen-SS units of troops who could claim some German ancestry (*Volksdeutsche*) and other foreign volunteers without ethnic Germanic origins (*Freiwilligen*) had a special unit collar patch created in lieu of the runes.

Collar *Tresse*

The SS collar *Tresse* were of the diamond Wehrmacht pattern and were required to be worn on all tunics (with the exception of camouflage tunics) and optional on overcoats. The *Tresse* were affixed to the forward and bottom edge of the collar on all tunics, and a subdued colour was optional on field uniforms. *Sigrunen* were always worn on the right, with the rank tab on the left collar. Officer's collar *Tresse* were outlined with a thin white or aluminum border. SS non-commissioned officers (SS-Unterscharführer to SS-Hauptscharführer) wore silver *Tresse* to denote their status as NCOs. For example, an SS-Sturmmann wore a black wool or felt inverted chevron on the left sleeve with silver NCO *Tresse* in the shape of a 'V', and two strips of sutash on their left collar tab, and SS-Rottenführer wore the same chevron on the left sleeve with the addition of a second NCO *Tresse* strip, with four strips of sutash on their left collar tab.

Sleeve Rank Insignia for unrated ranks

SS-Panzerobergrenadiers wore a black wool or felt circle containing a white or silver embroidered diamond on the left sleeve.

Vehicle Insignia

Adopted in 1940, the basic *Leibstandarte* vehicle insignia was a skeleton key (which translates into German as 'Dietrich'). In 1941 the key was enclosed in a shield, changed to a bevelled shield in 1943, and with the award of Oakleaves to Dietrich's Knight's Cross in 1944 these were added. There were also symbols and numbers to distinguish particular units.

PERSONAL IDENTIFICATION

Soldbuch

Each soldier carried at all times his *Soldbuch* (soldier's pay book) containing information such as place of birth, name, equipment numbers, pay records, leave

Above: An unnamed SS-Sturmmann of the LSSAH wearing shoulder straps with the prewar fourth, and final, pattern LAH cipher. This cipher dates this photo as been taken late in 1938 or early in 1939.

Above right: A tunic being examined by British field intelligence somewhere in Normandy, 1944. The cuff-band 'Adolf Hitler' together with the prewar, third-pattern shoulder strap with its distinctive pointed end clearly indicate an SS-Unterscharführer.

Right: A heavy artillery SS unit on coastal defence duty somewhere in France, October 1940. This photo clearly illustrates the distinctive helmet insignia carried, at least during the early part of the war, on the steel helmets of the Waffen-SS. Black runes on a white shield worn on the right side and a black swastika standing on its point set against a white disc within a red shield on the left. The red, white and black represented the then national colours of Germany and the Swastika the official emblem of both the Party and the German State. The chalk drawing of an umbrella is a reference to the former British Prime Minister, Neville Chamberlain who was frequently caricatured carrying an umbrella.

Left: SS-Hauptscharführer Hubert Walter wearing service dress with breeches.

papers, photo ID, money, mementos of home — pictures, letters of family, wives, girlfriends and memories of battles in which he had fought.

Identification disc

Every SS soldier was also issued identification discs, which he was required to wear suspended around his neck by a cord at all times. The oval zinc disc was divided by perforations. Information on the disc detailed the soldier's roster number, his unit, and his blood type. This information was duplicated on the other half of the disc, and in the event of death, the disc could be snapped in two. The portion with the cord stayed on the body and the other half went to his family.

Most, although not all, Waffen-SS troops also had their blood type tattooed under their left arm. The purpose of the tattoo was for medics to quickly determine a wounded man's blood type. After the war, Allied investigators used the tattoo to identify war crimes' suspects, prompting many SS members to burn or disfigure their skin to avoid capture. This only applied to ORs as officers were not obligated to get the tattoo.

Below and Bottom: Waffen-SS collar tabs for the rank of Sturmmann. The collar tabs usually featured the Nordic double-runes' symbol associated with the SS that were worn on the right-hand side. The SS drew heavily on Nordic symbology when creating their own system of ranks and associated insignias. The silver stripe denotes this particular rank; this was worn on the right side. *Peter V Lukacs WW2 Militaria AB*

UNIFORMS

Particularly in the latter stages of the war, the Waffen-SS had a great variety of different uniforms and equipment. Here I have focused on those particular to *Leibstandarte*. The black uniform was the most striking and part of its enduring image. Identical to that worn by the *Allgemeine-SS*, it consisted of black wool blouse, brown shirts, matching black tie, tapered trousers and high polished boots, worn with swastika armband, rank insignia, the honour cuffband, and a brown belt upon which ordinary troops attached three leather K98 ammunition pouches. NCOs and officers had a leather cross belt to support the sword scabbard carried on the left. In the mid-1930s a white belt and cross belt was substituted.

Although impressive as a parade uniform, it was not practical for use in the field, and in the summer of 1933 a grey-white cotton drill uniform was procured for the fledgling armed SS units. Commissioned officers' and NCOs' drill jackets were of similar cut to the original black tunic and were designed to incorporate both collar patches and shoulder straps. Non-rated soldiers were issued a tunic with standing collar, although it was not as finely tailored as those of officers and NCOs. In early 1935, an earth-grey uniform was adopted by the soldiers of the *Leibstandarte* and the SS-VT. The SS political armband was thought too striking for field use, and so it was replaced with the national emblem, which was worn on the left arm.

Field service blouse

In 1937, both the earth-grey and earth-brown uniforms were phased out as *Leibstandarte* switched to the field grey of the army. They were kitted out from army

Left: The M44 combat uniform in camouflage was used extensively in the Ardennes and Normandy. This squad leader carries the MP40 machine-pistol and a P38 pistol. He also has a hand grenade tucked into his belt behind the ammunition pouch for the MP40. *Wade Krawczyk*

Far left: Displayed on the cover of an original SS photo album impressed with the famous 'Double Runes' (*Doppelrunen*) is an SS officer's belt buckle; a Waffen-SS enlisted grade sleeve eagle; LAH officer's gilt shoulder strap cipher; enlisted rank's machine-woven cuff title bearing the signature 'Adolf Hitler'; uncut *Totenkopf* insignia for the field cap; and an enlisted grade belt buckle bearing the legend '*Meine Ehre heißt Treue*' (Loyalty is my honour!). *Peter V Lukacs WW2 Militaria AB*

Below: This Waffen-SS general's peaked cap (*Schirmmütze*) is piped in silver designating general officer rank. The silver chinstrap cords denote an officer. *Peter V Lukacs WW2 Militaria AB*

Right: The Führer salutes the troops of the *Leibstandarte* drawn up with their colour on the Berlin Lichterfelde parade ground. Hitler is accompanied (on his left) by SS-Obergruppenführer Sepp Dietrich.

Below right: Winter clothing — SS-Obergruppenführer und General der Waffen-SS Sepp Dietrich (wearing sheepskin coat) accompanied by senior divisional officers including SS-Obersturmbann-führer Kurt Meyer (on his left).

Below: An LSSAH guard of honour presents arms to Hitler during the 1938 Munich conference when the British Prime Minister, Neville Chamberlain, and the French Premier, Daladier, confronted Hitler and Mussolini. To appease Germany the fate of Czechoslovakia was sealed when, to all intents and purposes, large sections of the country were handed over to the Germans without consultation with the Czech government. Six months later the rest of Czechoslovakia was absorbed into the Greater German Reich.

stocks of M1936 pattern field grey jackets, to which were added SS insignia. In 1940, the distinctive dark green collar and shoulder straps of the SS were changed to field grey. A variation in 1942 was the discontinuation of pocket pleats as a labour and material saving measure, although material quality was already in decline. Further labour and material saving measures came in 1943, including the elimination of the pocket flap points and the internal suspenders, the use of rayon for the jacket lining and a 70/30 percent wool/cellulose blend for the new outer material, which also had less of a 'green' tint. The 1944 pattern tunic introduced changes to colour, now olive brown or '1944 field grey' and a reduction in the number of belt hooks to two. The design was tested and adopted for all German ground forces, including the Waffen-SS, in July 1944, although uniform material manufactured at this time of the war was very poor, in some cases containing 90 percent artificial fibres.

Officer's field service blouse

Officers of the Waffen-SS adopted field grey as their uniform colour at the same time as the other ranks — much the same as the army. However, the basic design was retained throughout the war. Key features were turnback cuffs, dark green pointed collar and scalloped pockets. Material quality fell dramatically during the war, and it was not unusual for officers' uniform to adopt modified enlisted mens' issue field blouses when their own kit wore out.

Field service trousers

The 1942 mountain-style trousers or *Keilhosen* were the most widely used trousers in the German Army after 1941, although less often used by the Waffen-SS, which continued to produce the M37 straight-leg service trousers. They have the same button-down loops to take a cartridge belt and trouser suspender hooks as the army version. The ankles taper and feature an adjustable stirrup to hold the trouser legs inside the gaiters.

Sturmartillerie/Panzer uniform

Tank and assault gun crewmen were issued with a uniform designed to be practical within the tight confines of an armoured vehicle. They were essentially of the same cut and made of black cloth. The blouson-style jacket was cut at the waist and fastened with a row of buttons arranged vertically on the right-hand side. The collar was large and worn open but could be fastened at the neck with a hook and eye. The trousers were tapered toward the ankles giving a bloused effect over boot top. The trousers had an integral belt and front pockets with pocket flaps. Standard insignia were worn on these uniforms.

Summer combat uniform

The need for a lighter, cooler uniform blouse for the summer prompted the SS to introduce its

own version of the Army's HBT field blouse, although it kept the traditional five-button front. The design remained the same throughout the war

Cold weather suits
These mouse-grey suits were actually the same as the German Army's cold weather suits introduced for the winter of 1942–43. The Waffen-SS had its own camouflage version of this uniform for the winter of 1943–44 which was identical in cut, except for slight stylistic changes to the pocket flaps. Various camouflage patterns were used.

Tropical uniforms
The Waffen-SS had a full line of uniform items for use in hot weather territory. These uniforms were used by Waffen-SS in Sardinia, Italy, Greece and Southern Russia.

Helmet (*Stahlhelm*)
The steel coal scuttle design dates back to the First World War and was standard issue for the infantry units. Painted in field grey it had a black leather chinstrap and air vent holes on the sides.

Footwear
Leibstandarte members were shod in the familiar German high marching boot, but by 1944–45 leather shortages meant that the boot been much reduced in height, and some new recruits were issued with a new style ankle boot, trialled by the German Army in 1935 and reintroduced in 1942. The

Left: This SS-Oberscharführer wears a reversible 'oakleaf' camouflage smock with a 'plane tree' pattern camouflage helmet cover. The Waffen-SS was innovative in the production and issue of camouflage clothing on a unit-sized basis. *Wade Krawczyk*

Right: *Soldbuch* for SS-Sturmmann Fritz Lederer. He wears the SS pattern Panzer wrap with the LAH cipher slides on his shoulder boards as a member of the 7th Company of Panzer Regiment 1. *Wade Krawczyk*

Below: Waffen-SS officer's sidecap. This sidecap belonged to Sturmbannführer Alfred Arnold, who wore it through the campaign in France and in Russia as a member of SS Infantry Regiment 9 and the *Totenkopf* Division. The front displays the SS pattern national eagle and the death's head (*Totenkopf*) badge. Arnold was killed in combat in October 1944. *Peter V Lukacs WW2 Militaria AB*

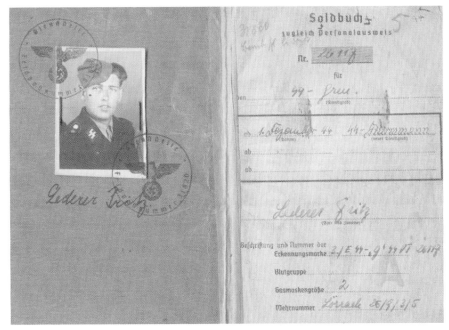

Below: This typical officer grade peaked cap (*Schirmmütze*) is piped in red designating artillery and displays the SS pattern national eagle and *Totenkopf*. The silver chinstrap cords denote an officer. *Wade Krawczyk*

Bottom : LAH cuff title. *Peter V Lukacs WW2 Militaria AB*

style varied; some were all eyeholes, others eyeholes and hooks. Heavy canvas gaiters were issued that provided the wearer with some ankle support, and also prevented stones and twigs getting into the boots. In the bitterly cold Russian winters, other types of lined boots such as those worn by Russian troops were a popular non-regulation alternative.

CAMOUFLAGE

Although it had been pioneered on ships and aircraft during World War I, the Waffen-SS was the first to use camouflage as an integral part of the soldier's standard combat uniform and equipment. A huge catalogue of camouflage patterns and styles for clothing, helmet covers and shelter tarps were developed. These camouflage items utilised by the Waffen-SS help one to distinguish the SS from the Wehrmacht, but it has to be noted that, due to late-war production shortages, many SS units also wore Italian or Wehrmacht camouflage items.

Camouflage smocks (*Tarnjacken*)
Two types of smock were issued, both of lightweight canvas or cotton duck material, and sometimes also waterproofed. All were reversible with a spring foliage pattern on one side and autumn foliage on the other. Multiple camouflage patterns were created during the war, of which the most recognisable are the 'oak leaf' (early war) and 'plane tree' (mid-war) patterns. There are countless others, details of which may be found in any comprehensive history of German uniforms. Other features of the smock were an elastic waistband, elastic cuffs, a drawstring front closure and shoulder loops to attach foliage. The first pattern had a shorter skirt than the second and also had two vertical slash-type openings on the left and right sides of the chest covered with a straight cut pocket flap. In 1943, while stationed in Italy, *Leibstandarte* seized vast amounts of Italian camouflage clothing, and this was later used to equip the 12th SS-Panzer Division *Hitler Jugend* and *Leibstandarte*'s own recruits. Italian-style camouflage fur anoraks are of much the same cut as the standard SS green fabric fur anorak, first used during the Ardennes offensive.

Camouflage helmet cover (*Stahlhelm Tarnüberzug*)
Made from the same material as the smock and reversible, the helmet cover was fastened to the sides and rear of the helmet by clips, and at the front by a reinforced lip of material overhanging the bill of the helmet. Sometimes loops were included for attaching foliage.

BASIC WAFFEN-SS FIELD EQUIPMENT

Black leather belt (*Koppel*) and belt buckle (*Koppelschloss*)
A black leather belt, 1.5 inches wide, was used for walking-out dress and for field use by all ranks. Brown belts were optional for officers. In addition to enhancing appearance, the belt was used to support the field equipment. Additional 'D' rings and leather equipment straps were also used to attach equipment to the belt.

Ammunition pouches (*Patronentaschen*)
The original Mauser Kar98K pouches were constructed of black leather, either sewn or riveted together, and worn in pairs. Attachments for the belt and 'Y' straps were provided. G43 pouches were constructed of a canvas material, with the same leather attachments for the belt as the K98 pouches, and could hold two 10-round magazines for the G43. Usually one of these pouches and one K98 pouch was worn on the belt.

Right: A member of the *Leibstandarte* captured near Trun seems almost relieved to have been taken prisoner by the Canadians. Although his pockets appear to have been searched, he still retains all his insignia.

Below right: SS volunteer from Bosnia and Herzegovina engaged in anti-partisan warfare, May 1944.

Below: Festooned with equipment, this Waffen-SS soldier is firing an aimed shot from his rifle. Although he is wearing all his issue equipment he is not wearing it in the prescribed manner — his mess tin is slung over his shoulder rather than attached to his belt; the water bottle is slung at left rather than at right; and his gas mask container is slung over the incorrect shoulder. It is unlikely that anyone other than a pedant would worry about this in the field!

MP40 pouches were similarly constructed of canvas with leather attachments for the belt and 'Y' straps, with capacity for three magazines per pouch. One of the pouches had an extra flap to hold the reloading tool. MP44 pouches were constructed of canvas, held three magazines per pouch and attached to the belt and 'Y' straps in the same fashion as the MP40 pouches.

In addition, machine gun crews carried an ammunition can and an MG belt loader, machine gunners' tool pouch (MG34 or MG42) and machine gun spare barrel carrier.

Bread bag (*Brotbeutel*)
The bag was constructed of heavy canvas, with attachments for securing it to the rear of the belt, in colours varying from olive drab to reed green. The flap had two leather straps for attaching the water bottle and/or mess tin. Eating utensils were usually carried in it, and a lard/butter container was also issued.

Water bottle (*Feldflasche*)
Constructed of aluminium, with a capacity of one litre, the covering of the *Feldflasche* was made of felt and the cup was large made of aluminium or smaller and made of bakelite. It was generally carried on the right side of the bread bag.

Yoke straps
Leather straps helped support the waist belt and field equipment, and were connected at the front to the back of ammunition pouches, and to the waist belt itself at the back.

Mess tin (*Kochgeschirr*)
For cooking and eating in the field, the mess tin could be carried on the 'Y' straps, small 'A' frame or the left side of the bread bag. Food was cooked on an Esbit stove.

Gas Mask Canister (*Tragebuhse*)
The distinctive fluted canister was usually strapped over the right shoulder, and the closed end had a retaining strap and hook to secure it to the waist belt.

Entrenching Tool
Both World War I and World War II pattern entrenching tools were carried by the Waffen-SS. Late war versions included a pick. It was carried in a leather pouch on the waist belt at the left hip.

Poncho/shelter quarter (*Zeltbahn*)
This was produced in waterproof materials of various camouflage patterns, with Spring/Summer on one side and Fall/Winter. on the other. It was variously used as a poncho, or shelter half, and rolled and either strapped to the "A" frame, or hooked to the yoke straps.

Bayonet, scabbard and frog (*Seitengewehr und Scheide*)
The standard issue bayonet was produced with both wooden and bakelite handles, and was carried in a scabbard suspended from the belt on the left hip. As an added measure of camouflage the scabbard was usually blued or painted flat black.

Optional equipment included an A frame for mounting equipment, a bag for personal items, flashlight, blanket, trench knife, goggles and gas cape bag. Depending on their needs officers, NCOs, artillerymen, field police and machine gun crews were issued map cases, binoculars, compasses and whistles (for signalling).

Right: This is an M40 combat tunic for an SS-Sturmmann. It displays the machine-woven cuff title of the LSSAH as well as the slip-on shoulder strap ciphers bearing the letters 'LAH'. Piping is in white for infantry. Until 1940 the Waffen-SS used the M1936 army uniform with a distinctive dark green collar and shoulder straps. After that date they dispensed with the coloured collar and straps, reverting to the Wehrmacht field grey. The M40 combat tunic was only superseded in 1942 — and then only in limited numbers — by a new combat tunic produced by the SS clothing works (*SS-Bekleidungswerkel*). Note the pleated pockets and *Hoheitsabzeichen* (national emblem) on the left sleeve. *Wade Krawczyk*

Right: Waffen-SS camouflaged Panzer wrap tunic. Intended as an overgarment or summer tunic, this example displays the 'dot' pattern camouflage used towards the end of the war. The only insignia is a subdued cloth sleeve eagle. *Wade Krawczyk*

Above left: The warning '*Abstand 30m*' (Stand back 30m) was a slogan peculiar to the motorised vehicles of the LSSAH. It was painted on the rear of all their vehicles on the express instructions of Sepp Dietrich as an aid to keeping safe distances between vehicles in convoy. Note also the skeleton key, the division's vehicle insignia.

Left: The Day of Fallen Heroes (*Heldengedanktag*), 21 March 1943. Adolf Hitler, accompanied by senior officers representing the Luftwaffe (Göring), the Kriegsmarine (Dönitz), the OKW (Keitel), the police (Himmler), together with Milch (Luftwaffe) and von Bock (Army). Drawn up in review order in front of the *Ehrenmal* — the World War I war memorial — the contingent nearest the camera is from the *Leibstandarte*-SS Adolf Hitler with their 1st Battalion colour.

Above and Above right: In order to operate in the open during the severe weather conditions warm clothing was essential. The Waffen-SS were frequently issued with better quality clothing and equipment — as seen here. The man on the left is wearing white single-piece snow overalls and pouches for his MP40 spare magazines.

Right: Massed 'Germany Awake' SS standards paraded at Nuremberg during the 1937 *Reichsparteitag*.

Above: Amongst the many flags and standards
captured by the victorious Soviet forces was the
standard of the 'Adolf Hitler' Regiment shown here,
minus its cloth banner, being carried by Russian
soldiers during the Victory Parade held in Moscow on
24 June 1945.

Above left: Paris, France, July 1942. Sepp Dietrich and
Generaloberst Haase (right), Commanding General of
the Fifteenth Army, inspect and admire the newly
produced, and unique, artillery guidon about to be
presented to a detachment of the LSSAH.

Left: The colour for the infantry battalion from LSSAH
being used for swearing-in new recruits at the division's
barracks, Berlin-Lichterfelde.

Right: Massed SS standards paraded during the seventh
Party Congress, the Party Day of Freedom, held at
Nuremberg from 10 to 16 September 1935. It was at
this congress, on 10 September, that the German
Citizenship Law and the Law for the Protection of
German Blood and German Honour — thereafter
known as the Nuremberg Laws — were proclaimed.
Flags and standards were of particular importance to
the Nazis, and used to great effect at the Nuremberg
rallies.

PEOPLE

JOSEF 'SEPP' DIETRICH

Undoubtedly the most celebrated of *Leibstandarte* soldiers was its founder, first and long-time commander Oberstgruppenführer Sepp Dietrich. Dietrich was born and raised in Bavaria, served as a sergeant-major in World War I, and after the war was attracted into the Freikorps volunteers. Subsequently he became a member of the SA and participated in the Munich Beer Hall Putsch. In 1928 he switched to the SS, and was one of the small group of bodyguards from which the *Leibstandarte* grew. Hitler expected and had their absolute loyalty, and after he had risen to power he called on Dietrich to formalise the unit. For more than 10 years Dietrich led the *Leibstandarte*, overseeing its growth from a tiny elite hand-picked ceremonial troop into the most feared of all the SS divisions. From his men he demanded excellence and gave in return genuine care and respect, which earned him their adulation and loyalty.

Below: Dietrich as an SS-Gruppenführer photographed just prior to his being promoted by Adolf Hitler to the rank of SS-Obergruppenführer.

The relationship between commander and men in *Leibstandarte* was far closer than in most of the Wehrmacht, but relations with his own superiors were often far less cordial. He had frequent and often bitter rows with Himmler, Reichsführer-SS, and it is unlikely that he would have achieved so much without the protection and patronage of the Führer himself. This friendship brought rapid promotion through the ranks of the SS; in the summer of 1943 he was appointed to create I SS-Panzer Corps. The army generals, von Rundstedt among them, tended to regard him as a good leader of men but a poor strategist, and his brusque manner, common roots and frequent use of gutteral German further alienated them. Perhaps, too, they were envious of the relationship between the Führer and the commander of his bodyguard, which was unique among German commanders, forged out of mutual respect between ex-comrades-in-arms and in the political struggle of the 1920s.

In 1944, Dietrich led I SS-Panzer Corps at Caen and was promoted to command the Sixth SS-Panzer Army for the Ardennes Offensive. His leadership earned him Swords & Diamonds to the Oak Leaves to the Knight's Cross he already had. But Dietrich's career was so peppered with accusations of atrocities — both real and imagined — that postwar saw him tried and convicted for war crimes. Many consider him lucky not to have been executed. When he was released from prison in 1956, he was still an unrepentant and committed Nazi, a firm adherent to the beliefs that he took with him to his grave in 1966.

OTTO KUMM

Kumm, the last commander of the *Leibstandarte*, was born in Hamburg on 1 October 1909, the son of a salesman. At the age of 21 he joined the Nazi Party and SS, and was a soldier in the SS-VT unit *Der Führer*. He rose through the ranks and at the close of the Western campaign as a SS-Hauptsturmführer was awarded the Iron Cross I and II Class. During service in Russia he won promotion to the command of the 4th SS-Panzergrenadier Regiment *Der Führer*, and in February 1942, as the regiment fought in the area of Rzeh Kumm, saw it reduced from 2,000 to 35 men. Subsequently he was awarded the Knight's Cross, and in April 1943 became Chief of Staff of the 5th Panzergrenadier Division *Wiking*. As SS-Oberführer Kumm, in August he took over command of 7th SS Freiwilligen Mountain Division *Prinz Eugen* from Carl von Oberkamp, and during his time with the unit was awarded Swords to the Knight's Cross he had already earned. In November came promotion to to SS-Brigadeführer und Generalmajor der SS and finally, in February 1945, command of 1st SS Panzer Division *Leibstandarte–SS Adolf Hitler*. In April came the Swords to his Knight's Cross, and a month later he surrendered with the remnants of the division. After the war he wrote the history of the 7th SS Division.

Above: Sepp Dietrich was the 41st recipient of the Oakleaves, awarded to him on 31 December 1941 for the part he played in the Balkans campaign as commander of the LSSAH. He was the first Waffen-SS officer to receive the Oakleaves. He is seen here in a SdKfz 251 command vehicle.

KURT 'PANZER' MEYER

After working as a miner and then serving with the Mecklenburg police, Meyer was attracted into the Nazi Party and joined the SS. In 1932 he was promoted to Untersturmführer and two years later as Obersturmführer was selected for the *Leibstandarte*. He served in Poland and France, gaining promotion to SS-Sturmbannführer, and was the commander of the reconnaissance detachment in Greece, where he led the spectacular assault on the Klissura Pass on 15 May 1941 (see page 26). In Russia he won the Oakleaves to his Knight's Cross at Kharkov and promotion to SS-Obersturmbannführer, and from there came command of the 25th SS-Panzergrenadier Regiment (12th SS-Panzergrenadier Division *Hitler Jugend*) as SS-Standartenführer. He led this unit through the early Normandy campaign, where

COMMANDING OFFICERS OF THE LEIBSTANDARTE

SS-Oberstgruppenführer Joseff Dietrich	1 September 1939	7 April 1943
SS-Brigadeführer Theodor Wisch	7 April 1943	20 August 1944
SS-Brigadeführer Wilhelm Mohnke	20 August 1944	6 February 1945
SS-Brigadeführer Otto Kumm	6 February 1945	8 May 1945

it bore most of the brunt of the early fighting and sustained enormous casualties. In August, following the death of *Hitler Jugend* commander Fritz Witt, he became at 33 the youngest divisional commander in the German Army. The following month he was captured near Amiens, and postwar was tried and sentenced to life imprisonment for the murder of Canadian prisoners in Normandy. In prison he wrote his memoir *Grenadiere* and was released after 10 years in jail. He died in 1961 a committed Nazi.

WILHELM MOHNKE

Mohnke, who has gained notoriety as the alleged perpetrator of the Wormhoudt and Malmédy massacres, was born in Lübeck in 1911. In 1931 he joined the NSDAP and the SS, served with the Lübeck troop, and then the 22nd SS Detachment, and in 1933 volunteered and was selected to form the core of the *Leibstandarte*. For the campaign in France, he was senior company commander of 2nd Battalion and reportedly ordered British POWs to be executed at Wormhoudt. In 1941, during the Balkans campaign, he lost a foot during an air attack and from 1943–44 was commander 26th Panzergrenadier Regiment, 12th SS-Division *Hitler Jugend*. He became commander of *Leibstandarte* in August 1944, a position he held until the following February. After leading the defence on the Seine, during the Ardennes Offensive Mohnke was accused of instigating the Malmédy massacre.

His final appointment was as commander of the Kampfgruppe Mohnke, tasked with the defence of the Reich Chancellery, and he was present in the Führerbunker when Hitler committed suicide. Captured by Soviets, he was finally released 1955, but despite efforts by the survivors of the massacres he has never been brought to trial.

JOACHIM ('JOCHEN') PEIPER

Joachim (he preferred Jochen, saying it sounded less Jewish) Peiper was, perhaps, the consummate SS hero. His wartime exploits made him at once a hero among ordinary Germans and a murderer to others. Born in 1915, at the age of just 19 he joined the SS-VT. His brothers were in the SS-TK and another in the SD. He went through two years of officer training and in 1936 was posted to the *Leibstandarte*. In 1938 he worked for a three-month long period as adjutant to Heinrich Hammer, during which time he worked with concentration camp commanders and, it is suggested, therefore had knowledge of plans for the Final Solution.

Peiper spent the first wartime campaign, in Poland, as part of Hitler's staff. He saw his first action with *Leibstandarte* in 1940, during the campaign for France. Here he led the assault on the Wattenberg heights and was awarded the Iron Cross 1st and 2nd class for his actions. For a long period he commanded the 3rd Battalion of SS-Panzergrenadier Regiment 2, and established an outstanding reputation as a combat leader. In 1943, he won the Knight's Cross at Kharkov for orchestrating the rescue of the 320th Infantry Division, which was then retreating to the Donets and in danger of being annihilated. Peiper took a small battle group deep into the Russian lines and extricated the survivors. In 1944, for the Ardennes Offensive, he was given his most famous command — SS-Kampfgruppe Peiper — and tasked with leading the spearhead of the German offensive. Subsequently promoted to

Above: SS-Obersturmbannführer Kurt Meyer, commanding officer of the 1st SS-Panzer Reconnaissance Battalion, LSSAH, photographed on the day he was awarded the Oakleaves to his Knight's Cross — 23 February 1943 — for actions on the Eastern Front. He became the 195th recipient of this award.

SS-Standartenführer, commanding SS-Panzer Regiment 1, he was the youngest regimental colonel in the Waffen-SS.

His name was implicated in massacres in Italy and at Malmédy, and postwar he was sentenced to hang. The sentence was commuted, and he was released from prison in 1956. Finding life in postwar Germany incompatible with his fervent Nazi beliefs, and its people intolerant of his past, in 1970 he moved to France. He was murdered at his home on Bastille Day in July 1976.

THEODOR WISCH

Born in 1907 in Wesselburener Hoog, 'Teddy' Wisch joined the *Leibstandarte* in March 1933 at the age of 25. A thoroughly professional soldier, if reportedly rather uncharismatic, he won rapid promotion through the ranks and by the start of the Polish campaign was a company commander. In Poland he won both the 1st and 2nd classes of the Iron Cross, and after serving in the Western, Balkans and Russian campaigns he was awarded the Knight's Cross in September 1941. The following summer he became commander of the 22nd SS-Panzergrenadier Regiment (part of the 10th SS-Panzer Division *Frundsberg*) and at Kharkov won the German Cross in Gold. In July 1943, at the age of 36, he took command of *Leibstandarte*, a position he held until the Normandy campaign when he was seriously wounded and invalided out. Awarded the Knight's Cross with Swords and Oakleaves, Wisch ended the war at a desk job in the SS-Fuhrüngshauptamt

MICHAEL WITTMANN

The most successful and decorated tank commander of the war, Wittmann was born in the rural Oberfalz region of Bavaria and first joined the regular army. In 1936, as a Gefreiter, he joined the SS-VT and was accepted into the 17th Company of the *Leibstandarte*, retaining the equivalent rank of SS-Mann. His initial training and service was on light reconnaissance vehicles, and at the outbreak of the war he was an SS-Unterscharführer in command of an armoured car. After the French campaign the regiment re-equipped with StuG III self-propelled guns, and Wittmann requested — and was granted — a transfer into the new detachment. Training on the new vehicles was completed in time for the Balkan campaign, in which he was awarded the 2nd class of the Iron Cross for his part in the assault on the Klissura Pass. During the summer, in Russia, he was awarded the 1st Class. Distinguishing himself further in the actions in the Crimea, at the end of 1942 Wittmann was sent to the SS officer training school at Bad Toldt and after passing out with the rank of Untersturmführer, he led the 13th (Heavy) Company of the 1st SS Panzer Regiment. At Kursk, on the first day alone, Wittmann destroyed eight enemy tanks and seven anti-tank guns, but his most famous action was at Villers-Bocage during the battle of Normandy in the West, when as SS-Obersturmführer he led the Tigers of his 2nd Company, SS-Panzer Abteilung 101, against a concentration of British armour threatening the *Panzer Lehr*, and destroyed 23 British tanks and a similar number of half-tracks and light armoured vehicles. Awarded the Swords to his Knight's Cross with Oakleaves for this action, Wittmann refused to accept a training post and was killed on 8 August 1944 in the fighting around Caen.

Below: Michael Wittmann sitting on the mantlet of his Tiger. Note the application of *Zimmerit* paste that produces the characteristic ridges appearance to later war images of German armoured vehicles. Zimmerit was designed to create a surface against which magnetic anti-tank weapons would not stick.
via George Forty

ASSESSMENT

In 1939, the SS-VT was not a favoured body. The army discouraged recruitment to it and, with the exception of *Leibstandarte*, numbers had to be made up from *Volksdeutsche*. In battle, however, the performance of the *Leibstandarte*, and the other elite SS divisions, gave rise to a very different notion: that they could save any situation and turn defeat into victory. Thus they were thrown into the most intense fighting time after time, and received preferential treatment with regard to supplies and equipment. Their feats encouraged Hitler to expand the Waffen-SS, and by 1944 it had swelled to an estimated 900,000 men. Something like 253,000 of these men were killed in action during the war, and an additional 250,000 wounded. But there existed very considerable variation in the quality of the SS divisions, many of which performed poorly in battle and in their treatment of 'enemies'. Appallingly, it is true to say that while the Waffen-SS and the seven elite divisions were among the best of German soldiers, they contained some of the worst characters.

Leibstandarte is considered the finest of the Waffen-SS divisions, and a myth has arisen around the unit that portrays it as a heavily armed army of six-foot blond, blue-eyed warriors charging into battle astride Tiger tanks like latter-day Teutonic Knights. This has more to do with the Nazi propaganda machine than the true facts, which are rather more complex. From its inception the *Leibstandarte* was supposed to represent the ideological elite of the 1,000-year Reich, the very epitome of the SS ideal, a Teutonic elite of physically perfect, impeccably bred specimens. Certainly, in the 1930s, when *Leibstandarte* could afford the luxury of stringent recruitment standards, the propaganda image was rather more accurate. But as war began to eat into Germany's manpower reserves, the SS began to recruit from rather more varied quarters. Although its recruitment standards remained high, the truth is that the men who fought and died under the banner of the Führer were a much more varied bunch. They may not have matched the exacting criteria Himmler set out for the SS at its

Below: Waffen-SS troops resting. While there is no doubt that atrocities committed by soldiers such as these were not uncommon, especially on the Eastern Front, there is also no doubting their qualities as fighting men.

inception but the demands made of them were never anything but superhuman.

Most accounts of the military history of the *Leibstandarte* inevitably focus on the most stunning battles or exciting campaigns. However, it is important to take a closer look at the combat records of the individual *Leibstandarte* to get a clearer picture of its military contribution of the SS during the war.

At the outbreak of the war, tactical command of the Waffen-SS was devolved to the OKH, while Himmler oversaw administration. During the Polish campaign *Leibstandarte* faced combat for the first time, eager to prove itself and disprove its critics in the army, which maintained a lofty contempt for SS troops. Unleashed on the battlefield, this eagerness resulted in high casualties, and while admiring their courage and recklessness, the army felt that overall the SS troops suffered from a combination of recklessness and lack of training. This may have been true, but SS officers countered that the army gave them the most difficult assignments with minimal support. Perhaps both allegations contained a grain of truth and during the invasion of the Low Countries and France *Leibstandarte* showed its true worth as a fighting unit.

Above: A PzKpfw III moves past dug-in Waffen-SS infantry on the Eastern Front. Bravery, endurance, skill — *Leibstandarte* and the elite SS units had all of this and Hitler came to expect the impossible from them.

Speed was one of the factors underpinning the tactics of Blitzkrieg, and as one of the limited number of motorised units available, *Leibstandarte* had a key role. First it advanced with lightning speed to Rotterdam, next into France where it prevented a French breakout and then audaciously broke through the British defensive perimeter at Wattan. During the advance to Paris, moving again at a breakneck pace at the spearhead of von Kleist's Panzer Group, the division was rushed to reinforce Army Group A, held up in front of the city, and helped force a breach through the defensive line. The successes continued as the *Leibstandarte* pushed into the south and bottled up the the French Army in the Alps. During the April 1941 invasion of Greece, there were several notable incidents; the storming of the Klissura Pass by Meyer's reconnaissance battalion, demonstrates graphically the motivation these men had for battle.

It was in Russia and the Ukraine that the *Leibstandarte* earned its enduring reputation for bravery and steadfastness. Here, during Operation 'Barbarossa' and the subsequent autumn and winter campaign, it made its most valuable commitment and finally won the respect of its peers. For the initial phase it again demonstrated the effectiveness of mobile forces on the battlefield, redeploying to counter attacks on the vulnerable flanks of the armoured thrust toward Rostov, and sealing off the Uman pocket despite concerted attempts to relieve it. For the action at Uman it won praise from Generalmajor Werner Kempf, and later in the year, after the advance through the southern Ukraine to Rostov, German Army General von Mackensen was moved to say of December, 'This truly is an elite unit.'

Already Hitler had begun to expect the impossible from the Waffen-SS. He refused to countenance withdrawal at Rostov, which resulted in heavy casualties for

LEIBSTANDARTE STRENGTHS	
Date	**Men**
January 1935	2,531
January 1936	2,650
January 1937	3,177
January 1938	3,607
December 1938	3,626
June 1941	10,796
December 1942	20,844
December 1943	19,867
June 1944	19,691
December 1944	22,000

Above: This photograph, taken somewhere on the Eastern Front, shows an SS despatch rider. He has picked up a Russian weapon .

Leibstandarte, and irrationally denied them adequate clothing for the first brutal winter on the steppes. The result was that in the spring, after further defensive battles around Dnepropetrovsk, the division had to be pulled back to France to be rebuilt. By now the battle-hardened core of the unit was beginning to wither, and it was forced by manpower shortages to accept recruits of a lower calibre. Later in the year it yielded more of its experienced NCOs and officers to the 9th SS-Division *Hohenstaufen*. From here on this cycle of events was repeated with increasing regularity, until by the end of the war the fallen were being replaced by young, barely trained conscripts and draftees.

Always instilled in the troops was the belief that they were the vanguard of the legions forging the new Nazi empire, and thus carrying the expectations of a nation. Above all was the SS creed of self-sacrifice for the glory of the Reich, loyalty to the Führer and the honour of death in battle. It should be remembered that most of the troops had grown up schooled in Nazism, believed in its tenets and held death in contempt. Even after the war, Joachim Peiper, who had joined the SS at 19, expressed his dismay at what he believed to be the selfishness and materialism of postwar Germany. Although it is often pointed out that Germany during the war was by no means united under the swastika, it is safe to say that *Leibstandarte* was Nazi to the core.

1943 was perhaps the high water mark for *Leibstandarte*. The number of SS divisions and corps multiplied, and it won a stunning victory at Kharkov that gave succour after the reversals of the winter months. Summer brought the turning point in fortunes, when at Kursk the combined weight of the *Leibstandarte*, *Das Reich* and *Totenkopf* panzer divisions, despite inflicting enormous losses on the Red Army, failed to make a decisive penetration of the Soviet defences. Defeat came not at the hands of superior generalship but by sheer weight of numbers and the enemy's seemingly endless capacity to absorb losses.

During the long, costly and doomed defence in the east, *Leibstandarte* rushed about the front, plugging gaps in the line, rescuing encircled troops and mounting stubborn counter-attacks. Time and again, *Leibstandarte* displayed a willingness to keep on fighting even when the tactical situation was hopeless, but local successes were undermined by the constant shortages of men and materiel, and despite their bravery, *Leibstandarte* could not stem the red tide.

Hitler was given to remark that 'troops like the SS have to pay the butcher's bill more heavily than anyone else' — and pay they did. With the Reich collapsing, the Führer gave the *Leibstandarte* increasingly unrealistic and impossible orders to attack or to defend to the last man — orders that, at least in the attack, it did not have the capacity to execute. In Normandy, again there were tactical victories, which succeeded in delaying the Allied advance to the homeland. As the spearhead for the Ardennes offensive, *Leibstandarte* showed that it had retained its legendary tenacity in the attack; a breakthrough came tantalisingly close for Peiper's column, only to be thwarted by fuel shortages. In spring 1945 came the final stand in Hungary, where *Leibstandarte* headed the death ride of the Sixth SS-Panzer Army attempting to save Hitler's last remaining fuel supply. Forced back under overwhelming odds, they were berated by the Führer, and ordered to remove the honour cuffbands that were such a source of pride.

Disillusioned and facing inevitable defeat, in these final days of the war *Leibstandarte* men were no longer fighting for National Socialism, for Germany, or for the Führer who, for all their sacrifices, had so callously abandoned them. Instead they transferred the loyalty that they had sworn to the Führer to their unit, their comrades and their commanding officers.

'. . . Our lack of understanding and inner rejection of everything we heard from "up there" or "back home" led us to accept only one last **Heimat**, one final homeland. That was our unit, our "little heap" of men.'

Leibstandarte troops as a whole earned a distinguished combat reputation during World War II, renowned for both stunning offensive victories, tenacious defensive operations and feats of bravery, courage and tactical brilliance for which some 58 of those who served won the Knight's Cross. This reputation is tempered to a large degree by the numerous atrocities carried out by members of the division, and by association with the SS. Without seeking to offer justification for the actions of the division, with the benefit of historical hindsight, it is important to place events in their proper context, and consider the Germany in which these troops were raised.

The average age of the troops was but 19 years old, and many of them had grown up knowing only Nazism. Of course, one should not imagine that *Leibstandarte* troops were simple fools who believed everything Hitler impressed upon them about the superiority of the Germanic races, the invincibility of the Reich and the destiny of the SS as the future master race, but belief in the honour of self-sacrifice bred a disdain for death that accounts for the enormous losses that the *Leibstandarte*, and the Waffen-SS, was able to sustain. It also offers a clue to the disdain SS men showed on occasion for the life of others.

All of the Waffen-SS divisions were to a greater or lesser degree complicit in acts of savagery against enemy troops and civilians. *Leibstandarte*, by no means the worst perpetrator, is by association with the SS and its own actions tainted. After the war Dietrich, Peiper and many others stood trial for these crimes and served sentence for them.

Below: Riflemen and machine gun crews await the order to move forward.

REFERENCE

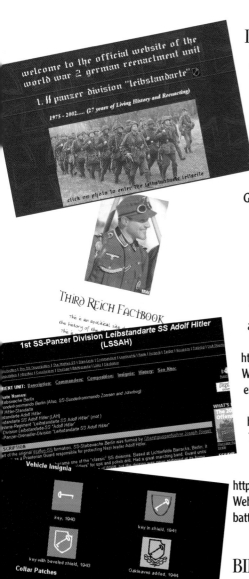

INTERNET SITES

The main problem with websites on *Leibstandarte*, the Waffen-SS or the SS in general is that they attract apologists of the Nazi cause, those who seek to shift the blame for atrocities away from military units onto unnamed individuals and political racists from the far right. We have not included here any websites that seem to us as being anything other than sites providing information of historical interest.

http://www.tankclub.agava.ru/sign/sign.shtml
Russian-language site with excellent illustrations of the tactical signs of the German armed forces.

http://www.geocities.com/Pentagon/3620/AchtungPanzer!
Site with very detailed information on German armour. Great colour pictures of preserved machines, particularly SPWs.

http://www.feldgrau.com/
This is probably the most comprehensive site dealing with the German Army before and during World War II currently on the Web. Well-written and researched.

http://www.lssah.com/
Website of 1st SS-Panzer Division re-enactors from US and Europe. The site emphasises its historical interests and that it is not political.

http://www.skalman.nu/third-reich/
The Third Reich Factbook — histories, orders of battle and other information on Third Reich military, political and volunteer organisations.

http://www.wssob.com/
Website that concentrates on the Waffen-SS. Plenty of information on history, orders of battle, etc.

BIBLIOGRAPHY

Bender, R. & Odegard, W.: *Panzertruppe – Uniforms, Organisation and History*; Bender, 1980. Panzer formations, crew uniforms and insignia, markings and camouflage.

Butler, Rupert: *SS-Leibstandarte The History of the First SS Division 1933-45*; MBI, 2001. Useful detailed history of the unit, particularly its more famous actions.

Culver, Bruce & Murphy, Bill: *Panzer Colours – Vol. 1*; 170 illustrations with 69 full-colour plates provide the most detailed account of German armour during WWII.

Delaney, John: *The Blitzkrieg Campaigns. Germany's 'Lighting War' Strategy In Action*; Arms & Armour Press, 1996. Describes the origins of the strategy developed during the interwar years; studies how this technique was used during the advances into Poland, Belgium and France then Russia.

Ellis, C. & Chamberlain, P.: *German Tanks and Fighting Vehicles of WWII*; Pheobus, 1976. This tells the story of German armour from the secret training machines of the Weimar period through to the end of WWII.

Erickson, John: *The Road To Stalingrad* and *The Road to Berlin*; Weidenfeld and Nicholson, 1983. Two volumes on Stalin's war with Germany, focusing on Soviet Command decisions.

Fomichenko, Maj-Gen: *The Red Army*; Hutchinson. Studies the development of the Soviet Army and its exploits from June 1941 when Germany launched Operation 'Barbarossa'.

Fugate, B.: *Operation Barbarossa: Strategy & Tactics 1941*; Spa Books, 1989. Studies Hitler's surprise offensive against Russia and analyses his strategy and tactics on the Eastern Front during 1941.

Glantz, David: *From The Don To The Dnieper*. Illustrations with detailed maps are included in this analysis of Red Army operations during eight vital months of struggle that finally ended Hitler's Blitzkrieg against the USSR.

Glantz, David: *Kharkov, 1942*; Ian Allan Publishing, 2000. A detailed appreciation of the battle with extensive quotations from the Soviet postwar study.

Gordon-Douglas, S. R.: *German Combat Uniforms 1939-45*; Altmark, 1970. Concentrates on combat equipment and field uniform.

Guderian, Heinz: *Achtung Panzer!* Classic book by one of the chief protagonists of armour in the 1940s details the development, tactics and operational potential of the German armoured forces and studies the evolution of land warfare and the years of German supremacy.

Haupt, Werner: *A History Of Panzer Troops 1916-1945*; Schiffer, 1990. An illustrated study of German armour from the Battle of Cambrai in 1916 to the 1944 Ardennes Offensive and the struggle to defend Berlin.

Jentz, Thomas L.: *Panzertruppen Vol 1 1933-1942*; *Vol. II – 1943-1945*; Schiffer, 1996. A complete guide to the creation, organisation and combat employment of Germany's Tank force 1933–45.

Above: A Waffen-SS machine gunner manages a smile despite the rain. He is wearing his shelter quarter (*Zeltbahn*) as a rain cape and, interestingly, over his helmet cover he is wearing a sniper's face mask, back to front, tied around the helmet.

Keegan, J.: *The Second World War*; Hutchinson, 1989. Excellent general history.

Keegan, J. (editor): *Encyclopedia of World War II*; Bison, 1980. A short, many-sided, history of the war as a whole. It includes biographies, details of major weapons, weapon systems, and details of all major battles. 1977.

Kershaw, Robert: *War Without Garlands*; Ian Allan, 2001. Excellent examination of Operation 'Barbarossa' and the battles of 1941.

Kessler, Leo: *The Life and Death of SS Colonel Jochen Peiper*; Leo Cooper/Secker & Warburg, 1986. Biography of this controversial figure.

Lederrey, Col E.: *Germany's Defeat in the East*; HMSO, 1955. A full account of the Soviet War against Germany during 1941–45.

Lucas, James: *War On The Eastern Front. The German Soldier in Russia 1941-1945*; Jane's, 1979. An account, from the German angle, of the war in the east.

Lucas, James: *Battle Group – German Kampfgruppen Actions of WWII*; BCA, 1994. The story of how Hitler's shock troops, the Kampfgruppen, contributed to German military operations.

Lucas, James: *The Third Reich*; Arms & Armour Press, 1990. A history of Germany's war through the words of German men and women who served with the armed forces or suffered from the devastation of Allied air raids.

Lucas, James: *The Last Year of the German Army* May 1944-May 1945; BCA, 1994. A complete study of structural changes to overcome its depletion and an insight into some of its last battles.

Lucas, James & Cooper, Matthew: *Hitler's Elite: Leibstandarte SS*; Macdonald and Jane's, 1975. Written over 25 years ago with the assistance of many veterans, this is a good account of the *Leibstandarte*, particularly on the unit character and motivation.

Lucas, James & Cooper, Matthew: *Panzer Grenadiers*; BCA, 1977. Excellent background on the panzergrenadier units, which were the first to combine motorised infantry with armoured fighting vehicles.

Mason, David. *Who's Who In World War II*; Weidenfeld and Nicholson, 1978. Presents a survey of the conflict told through the exploits of the main players who participated – military, political and scientific.

Mayer, S. L. (Editor): *Signal-Years Of Retreat 1943-44*; Bison, 1979. Hitler's wartime picture magazine. A facsimile edition of a propaganda journal supervised by Goebbels' propaganda company. A record of the decline and fall of the Third Reich.

Mclean, Donald B. (Editor): *German Infantry Weapons Vol I*; Normount Armament Co, 1967. Originally published in 1943 to assist Allied commanders, details the design and construction of weapons and their ammunition.

Messenger, Charles: *The Art of Blitzkrieg*; Ian Allan, 1995. Excellent discussion of blitzkrieg taking the story into the 1990s.

Messenger, Charles: *Hitler's Gladiator: The Life and Times of Oberstgruppenführer Und Panzergeneral-Oberst der Waffen-SS Sepp Dietrich*; Brassey's, 1988. Definitive biography of the legendary *Leibstandarte* commander.

Mollo, Andrew: *Army Uniforms of World War II*; Blandford, 1977. An easy reference and basic handbook on the uniforms, personal equipment and weapons of 24 nations that took part in WWII.

Pallud, Jean Paul: *Blitzkrieg In The West – Then And Now*; After the Battle, 1991. Fully illustrated Then and Now photographs show how Germany, in just sixty days, caused France to capitulate during 1941.

Piekalkiewicz, Janusz: *Operation Citadel*; Presidio, 1987. A complete illustrated analysis of the Battles of Kursk and Orel — the largest single land-air combat engagement in history which helped shatter Nazi ambitions in Russia.

Quarrie, Bruce: *Hitler – The Victory That Nearly Was*; David and Charles, 1988. An assessment of the situations which could have affected history had Hitler made different decisions, and won the war.

Rosignoli, Guido: *Army Badges and Insignia of World War II*; Blandford Press, 1972. Cap badges, formation signs, regimental badges, tank battle badges, shoulder sleeve insignia are all listed. Countries covered are Great Britain, USA, Italy, Poland, Belgium, and USSR.

Above: An obviously relaxed SS-Grenadier gives directions to a group of Soviet prisoners.

Scheibert, Horst & Elfrath, Ulrich: *Panzers in Russia*; Altmark, 1971. A pictorial record of the German Panzer divisions on the Eastern Front 1941–44. Over 400 pictures, with bi-lingual text, are shown in chronological order.

Seaton, Albert: *The German Army, 1933-1945*; Weidenfeld and Nicholson, 1982. A full length analytical study of the German Army, its rise and fall.

Warner, Philip: *Panzer*; Weidenfeld and Nicholson, 1977. This book gives a fascinating insight into the history of the Panzers. During the Second World War the power and success of these regiments were legendary.

Williamson, Gordon: The SS: Hitler's Instrument of Terror; MBI, 1994. Well illustrated informed general history of the rise and fall of the SS.

INDEX